MATHS
FRAMEWORKING

Complete success for Mathematics at KS3

YEAR 7

PUPIL BOOK 2

627345

KEITH GORDON   **KEVIN EVANS**   **BRIAN SPEED**

This chapter is going to show you

- some simple number patterns that you may have seen before, and how to describe them
- how to create sequences and describe them using some basic algebraic techniques
- how to generate and describe simple whole-number sequences

What you should already know

- Odd and even numbers
- Times tables up to 10×10

Sequences and rules

You can make up many different sequences with integers (whole numbers) using simple rules.

Example 1.1 ▶

Rule [add 3] Starting at 1 gives the sequence 1, 4, 7, 10, 13, …

Starting at 2 gives the sequence 2, 5, 8, 11, 14, …

Starting at 6 gives the sequence 6, 9, 12, 15, 18, …

Rule [double] Starting at 1 gives the sequence 1, 2, 4, 8, 16, …

Starting at 3 gives the sequence 3, 6, 12, 24, 48, …

Starting at 5 gives the sequence 5, 10, 20, 40, 80, …

So you see, with *different* **rules** and *different* **starting points**, there are very many *different* **sequences** you may make.

The numbers in a sequence are called **terms** and the starting point is called the **1st term**. The rule is often referred to as the **term-to-term rule**.

Exercise 1A

1 Use each of the following term-to-term rules with the 1st terms **i** 1 and **ii** 5.

Create each sequence with 5 terms in it.

a add 3	**b** multiply by 3	**c** add 5	**d** multiply by 10
e add 9	**f** multiply by 5	**g** add 7	**h** multiply by 2
i add 11	**j** multiply by 4	**k** add 8	**l** add 105

2 Give the next two terms in each of these sequences. Describe the term-to-term rule you have used.

   a   2, 4, 6, ...   **b**   3, 6, 9, ...   **c**   1, 10, 100, ...   **d**   1, 2, 4, ...

   e   2, 10, 50, ...   **f**   0, 7, 14, ...   **g**   7, 10, 13, ...   **h**   4, 9, 14 , ...

   i   4, 8, 12, ...   **j**   9, 18, 27, ...   **k**   12, 24, 36, ...   **l**   2, 6, 18 , ...

3 For each pair of numbers find at least two sequences, writing the next two terms. Describe the term-to-term rule you have used.

   a   1, 4, ...   **b**   3, 7, ...   **c**   2, 6, ...

   d   3, 6, ...   **e**   4, 8, ...   **f**   5, 15, ...

4 Find at least one sequence between each pair of numbers, fully describing the term-to-term rule you have used.

   a   1, ..., 8   **b**   1, ..., 12   **c**   5, ..., 15

   d   4, ..., 10   **e**   10, ..., 20   **f**   16, ..., 20

5 **i**   Make up some of your own sequences and describe them.

    ii   Give your sequences to someone else and see if they can find out what your term-to-term rule is.

Extension Work

1   Choose a target number, say 50, and try to write a term-to-term rule which has 50 as one of its terms.

2   See how many different term-to-term rules you can find with the same 1st term that get to the target number. (Try to find at least five.)

Finding missing terms

In any sequence, you will have a 1st term, 2nd term, 3rd term, 4th term and so on.

Example 1.2 ▶

In the sequence 3, 5, 7, 9, ..., what is the 5th term, and what is the 50th term?

You first need to know what the term-to-term rule is. You can see that you add 2 from one term to the next:

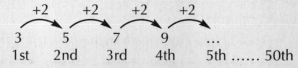

To get to the 5th term, you add 2 to the 4th term, which gives 11.

To get to the 50th term, you will have to add on 2 a total of 49 times (50 – 1) to the first term, 3. This will give $3 + 2 \times 49 = 3 + 98 = 101$

Exercise 1B

1 In each of the following sequences, find the 5th and the 50th term.

   a   4, 6, 8, 10, ...   **b**   1, 6, 11, 16, ...   **c**   3, 10, 17, 24, ...

   d   5, 8, 11, 14, ...   **e**   1, 5, 9, 13, ...   **f**   2, 10, 18, 26, ...

   g   20, 30, 40, 50, ...   **h**   10, 19, 28, 37, ...   **i**   3, 9, 15, 21, ...

2 In each of the sequences below, find the 1st term, then find the 50th term.

In each case, you have been given the 4th, 5th and 6th terms.
 a   ..., ..., ..., 13, 15, 17, ...
 b   ..., ..., ..., 18, 23, 28, ...
 c   ..., ..., ..., 19, 23, 27, ...
 d   ..., ..., ..., 32, 41, 50, ...

3 In each of the following sequences, find the missing terms and the 50th term.

Term	1st	2nd	3rd	4th	5th	6th	7th	8th	50th
Sequence A	...	...	...	...	17	19	21	23	...
Sequence B	...	9	...	19	...	29	...	39	...
Sequence C	...	...	16	23	...	37	44	...	...
Sequence D	...	...	25	...	45	...	...	75	...
Sequence E	...	5	...	11	...	...	20	...	...
Sequence F	...	...	12	...	...	18	...	22	...

4 Find the 40th term in the sequence with the term-to-term rule ADD 5 and a 1st term of 6.

5 Find the 80th term in the sequence with the term-to-term rule ADD 4 and a 1st term of 9.

6 Find the 100th term in the sequence with the term-to-term rule ADD 7 and 1st term of 1.

7 Find the 30th term in the sequence with the term-to-term rule ADD 11 and 1st term of 5.

Extension Work

1   You have a simple sequence where the 50th term is 349, the 51st is 354 and the 52nd is 359. Find the 1st term and the 100th term.

2   You are laying a new path in the park using this pattern.

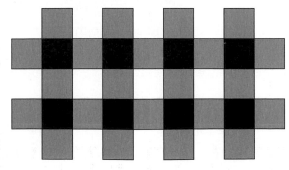

If you still have 50 black slabs, how many yellow slabs do you need now?

Finding the general term (*n*th term)

We can describe a sequence by finding the **nth term**. This is the **generalisation** that will allow us to find any specific term we want.

Example 1.3 ▷

Look at the sequence with the following pattern.

Pattern (term) number   1   2   3

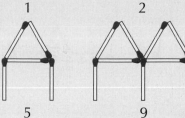 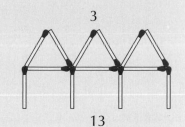

Number of matchsticks   5   9   13

a   Find the generalisation (*n*th term) of the pattern.

b   Find the 50th term in this sequence.

What is the term-to-term rule here? It is add 4, so the rule is based on **4*n***.

This 1st term is 5. Adding 4 gives the 2nd term, $5 + 4 = 9$, which could be written as $4 + 4 + 1 = 2 \times 4 + 1$. For the 2nd term, $n = 2$, which means that the generalisation is:

nth term = 4n + 1

You can use this to find the 50th term in the pattern.

When $n = 50$, $4n + 1 = 4 \times 50 + 1 = 201$

Exercise 1C

Find the generalisation (nth term) for the number of matchsticks in each of the following patterns.

Use this generalisation to find the 50th term in each pattern.

1

2

3

4

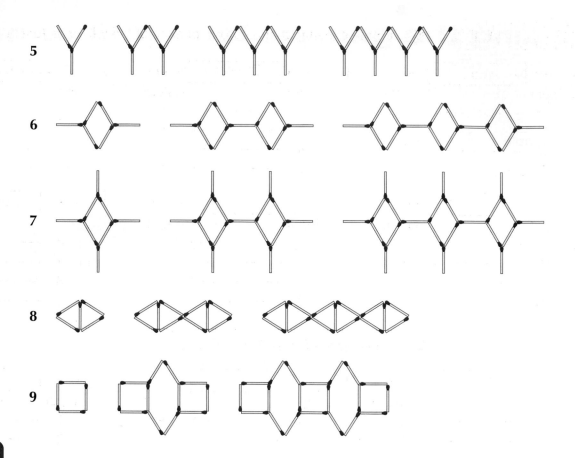

5

6

7

8

9

Extension Work

1   Make up some of your own patterns and find their generalisations.

2   Try creating patterns which have the generalisations:
   i $5n$ **ii** $5n + 1$ **iii** $3n + 2$ **iv** $4n + 3$

3   We haven't seen many generalisations with a negative number. Try to create a pattern that has the generalisation of $4n - 1$.

Functions and mappings

Example 1.4 ▷

Complete the function machine to show the output.

$\longrightarrow$ | multiply by 2 | $\longmapsto$ | add 5 | $\longrightarrow$

Input

3	... $\times 2 = 6$	$+5$	$=$	?
5	... $\times 2 = 10$	$+5$	$=$	?
7	... $\times 2 = 14$	$+5$	$=$	?

Output

The output box can be seen to be

| 11 |
| 15 |
| 19 |

1 Complete the input and output for each of the following function machines.

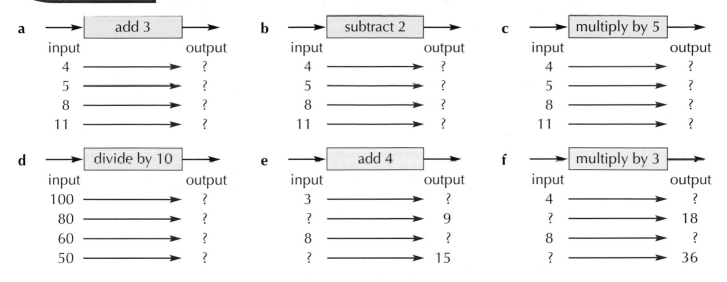

a input: add 3 → output
- 4 → ?
- 5 → ?
- 8 → ?
- 11 → ?

b input: subtract 2 → output
- 4 → ?
- 5 → ?
- 8 → ?
- 11 → ?

c input: multiply by 5 → output
- 4 → ?
- 5 → ?
- 8 → ?
- 11 → ?

d input: divide by 10 → output
- 100 → ?
- 80 → ?
- 60 → ?
- 50 → ?

e input: add 4 → output
- 3 → ?
- ? → 9
- 8 → ?
- ? → 15

f input: multiply by 3 → output
- 4 → ?
- ? → 18
- 8 → ?
- ? → 36

2 Express each of these functions in words.

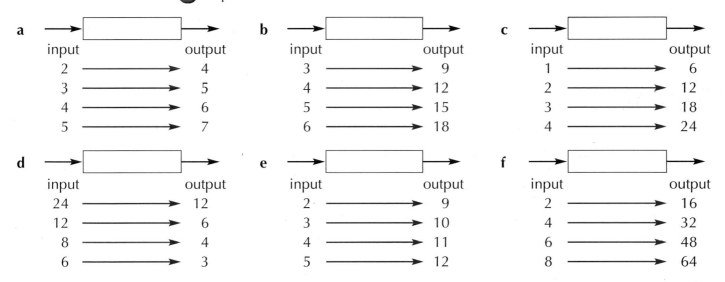

a input → output
- 2 → 4
- 3 → 5
- 4 → 6
- 5 → 7

b input → output
- 3 → 9
- 4 → 12
- 5 → 15
- 6 → 18

c input → output
- 1 → 6
- 2 → 12
- 3 → 18
- 4 → 24

d input → output
- 24 → 12
- 12 → 6
- 8 → 4
- 6 → 3

e input → output
- 2 → 9
- 3 → 10
- 4 → 11
- 5 → 12

f input → output
- 2 → 16
- 4 → 32
- 6 → 48
- 8 → 64

3 Draw diagrams to illustrate each of the following functions.

Start with any numbers you like for the inputs. But remember, the larger the numbers the more difficult the problems are to work out.

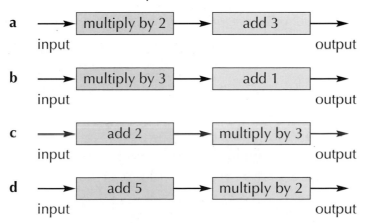

a input → multiply by 2 → add 3 → output

b input → multiply by 3 → add 1 → output

c input → add 2 → multiply by 3 → output

d input → add 5 → multiply by 2 → output

4 Each of the following functions is made up from two operations, as above.

Find the **combined functions** in each case.

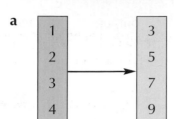 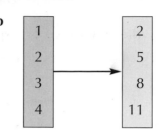 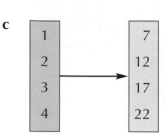

Extension Work

1 Work backwards from each output to find the input to each of the following functions.

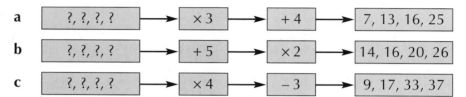

a ?, ?, ?, ? → × 3 → + 4 → 7, 13, 16, 25

b ?, ?, ?, ? → + 5 → × 2 → 14, 16, 20, 26

c ?, ?, ?, ? → × 4 → − 3 → 9, 17, 33, 37

2 From the following single functions, see how many different combined functions you can make.

| × 3 | + 4 | − 1 | × 2 | + 5 |

Using letter symbols to represent functions

Here is some algebra shorthand that is useful to know:

$2x$ means two multiplied by x

$2g$ means two multiplied by g

$5h$ means five multiplied by h

The idea of algebra is that we use a letter to represent a situation where we don't know a number (value) or where we know the value can vary (be lots of different numbers).

Each of the above is an **expression**. An expression is often a mixture of letters, numbers and signs. We call the letters **variables**, because the values they stand for vary.

For example, $3x$, $x + 5$, $2x + 7$ are expressions, and x is a variable in each case.

When the variable in an expression is a particular number, the expression has a particular value.

For example, in the expression $x + 6$, when $x = 4$, the expression has the value $4 + 6$, which is 10.

1 Write down what the expression $n + 5$ is equal to when:

   i $n = 3$ **ii** $n - 7$ **iii** $n = 10$ **iv** $n = 2$ **v** $n = 21$

2 Write down what the expression $3n$ is equal to when:

   i $n = 4$ **ii** $n = 8$ **iii** $n = 11$ **iv** $n = 5$ **v** $n = 22$

3 Write down what the expression $x - 1$ is equal to when:

   i $x = 8$ **ii** $x = 19$ **iii** $x = 100$ **iv** $x = 3$ **v** $x = 87$

4 Write each of the following rules in symbolic form: for example, $x \rightarrow x + 4$

   a add 3   **b** multiply by 5   **c** subtract 2   **d** divide by 5

5 Draw mapping diagrams to illustrate each of the following functions.

   a $x \rightarrow x + 2$ **b** $x \rightarrow 4x$ **c** $x \rightarrow x + 5$ **d** $x \rightarrow x - 3$

6 Express each of the following functions in symbols as in Question 4.

a
$2 \rightarrow 9$
$3 \rightarrow 10$
$4 \rightarrow 11$
$5 \rightarrow 12$

b
$2 \rightarrow 10$
$3 \rightarrow 15$
$4 \rightarrow 20$
$5 \rightarrow 25$

c
$2 \rightarrow 1$
$3 \rightarrow 2$
$4 \rightarrow 3$
$5 \rightarrow 4$

d
$2 \rightarrow 8$
$3 \rightarrow 12$
$4 \rightarrow 16$
$5 \rightarrow 20$

e
$12 \rightarrow 4$
$15 \rightarrow 5$
$21 \rightarrow 7$
$30 \rightarrow 10$

f
$2 \rightarrow 7$
$3 \rightarrow 8$
$4 \rightarrow 9$
$5 \rightarrow 10$

g
$2 \rightarrow 20$
$3 \rightarrow 30$
$4 \rightarrow 40$
$5 \rightarrow 50$

h
$12 \rightarrow 9$
$13 \rightarrow 10$
$14 \rightarrow 11$
$15 \rightarrow 12$

7 Draw mapping diagrams to illustrate each of these functions.

   a $x \rightarrow 2x + 3$ **b** $x \rightarrow 3x - 2$ **c** $x \rightarrow 5x + 1$ **d** $x \rightarrow 10x - 3$

8 Describe each of the following mappings as functions in the symbolic form, as above.

a
$1 \rightarrow 1$
$2 \rightarrow 3$
$3 \rightarrow 5$
$4 \rightarrow 7$

b
$1 \rightarrow 7$
$2 \rightarrow 11$
$3 \rightarrow 15$
$4 \rightarrow 19$

c
$1 \rightarrow 1$
$2 \rightarrow 4$
$3 \rightarrow 7$
$4 \rightarrow 10$

d
$1 \rightarrow 11$
$2 \rightarrow 21$
$3 \rightarrow 31$
$4 \rightarrow 41$

Think about a group of people who meet and want to shake each other's hands.

One person alone would have no one to shake hands with.

Two people would shake hands just once.

Three people would have three handshakes altogether.

Four people would have six handshakes altogether.

a Draw a simple diagram to represent these cases and so predict how many handshakes there will be with five people in the group.

b Put your results into a table and write any number sequences you see.

c Find the rule linking the number of people and the number of handshakes. Write this rule as a function.

A function investigation

Every two-digit whole number can be written as $10a + b$.

For example, $28 = 10 \times 2 + 8$.

Consider the function $\boxed{10x + y \rightarrow 10y - x}$

$36 \rightarrow 60 - 3 \rightarrow 57$
$19 \rightarrow 90 - 1 \rightarrow 89$
$75 \rightarrow 50 - 7 \rightarrow 43$

1 Start with any two-digit number, and make a chain out of the successive results until you get a repeated number. You have found a loop.
For example:

$\boxed{17} \rightarrow 70 - 1 \rightarrow \boxed{69} \rightarrow 90 - 6 \rightarrow \boxed{84} \rightarrow 40 - 8 \rightarrow \boxed{32} \rightarrow 20 - 3 \rightarrow \boxed{17}$

We start and finish with 17. Hence, we have the loop of 17.

Warning: If you ever have a result which is *not* a two-digit number, then you cannot have a loop – so you stop.

2 Find at least six of these loops.
Describe what you have noticed about each loop.

3 Do you think this will happen with every two-digit number?
Explain your answer.

4 What happens if you change the function to $\boxed{10x + y \rightarrow 9y - x}$?
Describe what happens.

5 Try other changes. Describe what you notice.

National Curriculum SATs questions

LEVEL 4

1 *1998 Paper 2*

Owen has some tiles like these:

He uses the tiles to make a series of patterns.

Pattern number
1

Pattern number
2

Pattern number
3

Pattern number
4

a Each new pattern has more tiles than the one before. The number of tiles goes up by the same amount each time.

How many more tiles does Owen add each time he makes a new pattern?

b How many tiles will Owen need altogether to make pattern number 6?

c How many tiles will Owen need altogether to make pattern number 9?

d Owen uses 40 tiles to make a pattern. What is the number of the pattern he makes?

2 *2000 Paper 2*

    a   Write down the next two numbers in the sequence below.

           281, 287, 293, 299, …, …

    b   Write down the next two numbers in the sequence below.

           1, 4, 9, 16, 25, …, …

    c   Describe the pattern in part **b** in your own words.

LEVEL 5

3 *2000 Paper 2*

You can make 'huts' with matches.

 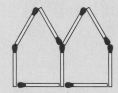 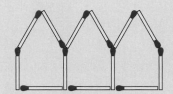

    1 hut needs   2 huts need   3 huts need
    5 matches   9 matches   13 matches

A rule to find how many matches you need is

$$m = 4h + 1$$

m stands for the number of matches

h stands for the number of huts.

    a   Use the rule to find how many matches you need to make 8 huts.
         (Show your working.)

    b   I use 81 matches to make some huts. How many huts do I make?
         (Show your working.)

This chapter is going to show you	What you should already know
○ how to work with decimals and whole numbers ○ how to use estimation to check your answers ○ how to solve problems using decimals and whole numbers, with and without a calculator	○ How to write and read whole numbers and decimals ○ How to write tenths and hundredths as decimals ○ Times tables up to 10×10 ○ How to use a calculator to do simple calculations

Decimals

Look at this picture. What do the decimal numbers mean? How would you say them?

When you multiply by 100, all the digits are moved two places to the left.

Example 2.1 ▷ Work out 3.5×100.

Thousands	Hundreds	Tens	Units	Tenths	Hundredths	Thousandths
			3 .	5		
	3	5	0 .			

The digits move one place to the left when you multiply by 10, and three places to the left when you multiply by 1000.

When you divide by 1000, all the digits move three places to the right.

Example 2.2 ▶

Work out 23 ÷ 1000.

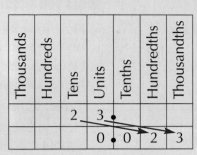

Thousands	Hundreds	Tens	Units	Tenths	Hundredths	Thousandths
		2	3.			
			0.	0	2	3

In the same way, the digits move one place to the right when you divide by 10, and two places to the right when you divide by 100.

Exercise 2A

1 Without using a calculator work out:

a	34 × 10	**b**	4.5 × 10	**c**	0.6 × 10	**d**	89 × 100
e	5.3 × 100	**f**	0.03 × 100	**g**	4 × 1000	**h**	5.8 × 1000
i	34 ÷ 10	**j**	4.5 ÷ 10	**k**	0.6 ÷ 10	**l**	89 ÷ 100
m	5.3 ÷ 100	**n**	4 ÷ 1000	**o**	58 ÷ 1000	**p**	0.04 ÷ 10
q	0.7 × 1000	**r**	7 ÷ 100	**s**	5.01 ÷ 10	**t**	6.378 × 100

2 Fill in the missing operation in each case.

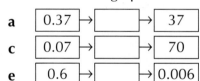

a 0.37 → [ ] → 37

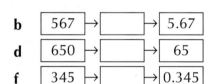

b 567 → [ ] → 5.67

c 0.07 → [ ] → 70

d 650 → [ ] → 65

e 0.6 → [ ] → 0.006

f 345 → [ ] → 0.345

3 Find the missing number in each case.

a 3 × 10 = ☐

b 3 × ☐ = 300

c 3 ÷ 10 = ☐

d 3 ÷ ☐ = 0.03

e 0.3 × 10 = ☐

f 0.3 × ☐ = 300

g 0.3 ÷ 10 = ☐

h 0.3 ÷ ☐ = 0.003

i ☐ ÷ 100 = 0.03

j ☐ ÷ 10 = 30

k ☐ × 1000 = 30 000

l ☐ × 10 = 300

4 Copy, complete and work out the total of this shopping bill:

1000 chews at £0.03 each =

100 packets of mints at £0.23 each =

10 cans of pop at £0.99 each =

Extension Work

Design a poster to explain clearly how to multiply and/or divide a number by 10, 100 or 1000.

Ordering decimals

Name	Leroy	Myrtle	Jack	Baby Jane	Alf	Doris
Age	37.4	21	$32\frac{1}{2}$	9 months	57	68 yrs 3 mths
Height	170 cm	1.54 m	189 cm	0.55 m	102 cm	1.80 m
Weight	75 kg	50.3 kg	68 kg	7.5 kg	85 kg	76 kg 300 g

Look at the people in the picture. How would you put them in order?

When you compare the size of numbers, you have to consider the **place value** of each digit.

It helps if you fill in the numbers in a table like the one shown on the right.

The decimal point separates the whole-number part of the number from the decimal-fraction part.

Thousands	Hundreds	Tens	Units	Tenths	Hundredths	Thousandths
			2	3	3	0
			2	0	3	0
			2	3	0	4

Example 2.3 ▷

Put the numbers 2.33, 2.03 and 2.304 in order, from smallest to largest.

The numbers are shown in the table. Zeros have been added to make up the missing decimal places.

Working across the table from the left, you can see that all of the numbers have the same units digit. Two of them have the same tenths digit, and two have the same hundredths digit. But only one has a digit in the thousandths. The order is

2.03, 2.304 and 2.33

Example 2.4 ▷

Put the correct sign, > or <, between each of these pairs of numbers:

a 6.05 and 6.046 **b** 0.06 and 0.065.

a Both numbers have the same units and tenths digits, but the hundredths digit is bigger in the first number. So the answer is 6.05 > 6.046.

b Both numbers have the same units, tenths and hundredths digits, but the second number has the bigger thousandths digit, as the first number has a zero in the thousandths. So the answer is 0.06 < 0.065.

1 a Copy the table on page 15 (but not the numbers). Write the following numbers in the table, placing each digit in the appropriate column.

4.57, 45, 4.057, 4.5, 0.045, 0.5, 4.05

b Use your answer to part **a** to write the numbers in order from smallest to largest.

2 Write each of these sets of numbers in order from smallest to largest.

a 0.73, 0.073, 0.8, 0.709, 0.7

b 1.203, 1.03, 1.405, 1.404, 1.4

c 34, 3.4, 0.34, 2.34, 0.034

3 Put the correct sign, > or <, between each of these pairs of numbers.

a 0.315 0.325   **b** 0.42 0.402   **c** 6.78 6.709

d 5.25 km 5.225 km   **f** 0.345 kg 0.4 kg   **g** £0.05 7p

4 Put these amounts of money in order.

a 56p £1.25 £0.60 130p £0.07

b £0.04 £1.04 101p 35p £0.37

5 Put these times in order: 1hour 10 minutes, 25 minutes, 1.25 hours, 0.5 hours.

6 One metre is 100 centimetres. Change all the lengths below to metres and then put them in order from smallest to largest.

6.25 m, 269 cm, 32 cm, 2.7 m, 0.34 m

7 One kilogram is 1000 grams. Change all the weights below to kilograms and then put them in order from smallest to largest.

467 g, 1.260 kg, 56 g, 0.5 kg, 0.055 kg

8 Write each of the following statements in words.

a 3.1 < 3.14 < 3.142

b £0.07 < 32p < £0.56

Extension Work

Choose a set of five consecutive integers (whole numbers), such as 3, 4, 5, 6, 7.

Use a calculator to work out the **reciprocal** of each of the five numbers. The reciprocal is the number divided into 1. That is:

1 ÷ 3, 1 ÷ 4, 1 ÷ 5, 1 ÷ 6, 1 ÷ 7

Put the answers in order from smallest to largest.

Repeat with any five two-digit whole numbers, such as 12, 15, 20, 25, 30.

What do you notice?

Directed numbers

Temperature 32 °C
Latitude 17° South
Time 09 30 h GMT

Temperature –13 °C
Latitude 84° North
Time 23 24 h GMT

Look at the two pictures. What are the differences between the temperatures, the latitudes and the times?

All numbers have a sign. Positive numbers have a + sign in front of them although we do not always write it. Negative (or minus) numbers have a – sign in front of them. We *always* write the negative sign.

The positions of positive and negative numbers can be put on a number line, as below.

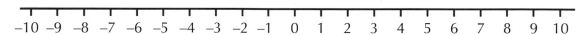

This is very useful, as it helps us to compare positive and negative numbers and also to add and subtract them.

Example 2.5 ▷

Which is bigger, –7 or –3?

Because –3 is further to the right on the line, it is the larger number. We can write $-7 < -3$.

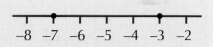

Example 2.6 ▷

Work out the answers to **a** $3 - 2 - 5$ **b** $-3 - 5 + 4 - 2$

a Starting at zero and 'jumping' along the number line give an answer of –4.

b $-3 - 5 + 4 - 2 = -6$

Example 2.7 ▷

Work out the answers to **a** $-2 - +4$ **b** $-6 - -3 + -2$

a Rewrite as $-2 - 4$ and count along a number line $-2 - 4 = -6$

b Rewrite as $-6 + 3 - 2$ and count along a number line $-6 + 3 - 2 = -5$

Exercise 2C

1 Put the correct sign, > or <, between each pair of numbers.

a $-5 \dots 4$ **b** $-7 \dots -10$ **c** $3 \dots -3$ **d** $-12 \dots -2$

2 Find the number that is halfway between each pair of numbers.

a $-8 \quad -2$ **b** $-6 \quad +3$ **c** $-9 \quad -1$

3 Work out the answer to each of these.

a $6 - 9$ **b** $4 - 3$ **c** $2 - 7$ **d** $3 + 9$ **e** $1 - 3$ **f** $4 - 4$
g $-6 + 9$ **h** $-4 - 1$ **i** $-7 - 3$ **j** $-1 + 8$ **k** $-2 - 3$ **l** $-14 + 7$
m $-2 - 3 + 4$ **n** $-1 + 1 - 2$ **o** $-3 + 4 - 7$ **p** $-102 + 103 - 5$

4 Copy each of these calculations and then fill in the missing numbers.

a
3 + +1 = 4
3 + 0 = 3
3 + −1 = 2
3 + −2 = ...
3 + ... = ...
3 + ... = ...

b
−2 − +1 = −3
−2 − 0 = −2
−2 − −1 = −1
−2 − −2 = ...
−2 − ... = ...
−2 − ... = ...

c
4 − +2 = 2
3 − +1 = 2
2 − 0 = 2
1 − −1 = ...
0 − ... = ...
... − ... = ...

5 Work out the answer to each of these.

a +3 − +2 **b** −4 − −3 **c** +7 − −6 **d** −7 + −3 **e** +7 − +3

f −9 − −5 **g** −6 + +6 **h** +6 − −7 **i** −6 + −6 **j** −1 + −8

k +5 − +7 **l** 7 − −5 **m** −2 − −3 + −4 **n** − +1 + +1 − +2

6 Find the missing number to make each of these true.

a +2 + −6 = ☐

b +4 + ☐ = +7

c −4 + ☐ = 0

d +5 + ☐ = −1

e +3 + +4 = ☐

f ☐ − −5 = +7

g ☐ − +5 = +2

h +6 + ☐ = 0

i ☐ − −5 = −2

j +2 + −2 = ☐

k ☐ − +2 = − 4

l −2 + −4 = ☐

7 **a** A fish is 10 m below the surface of the water. A fish eagle is 15 m above the water. How many metres must he descend to get the fish?

b Alf has £25 in the bank. He writes a cheque for £35. How much has he got in the bank now?

8 In a magic square, the numbers in any row, column or diagonal add up to give the same answer. Copy and complete each of these magic squares.

a

−7	0	−8
−2		−3

b

−2		−4
		−3
		−8

c

0		−13	−3
	−5		
−7	−9	−10	
−12			−15

Estimates

UNITED v CITY

CROWD	41 923
SCORE	2 – 1
TIME OF FIRST GOAL	42 min 13 sec
PRICE OF A PIE	95p
CHILDREN	33% off normal ticket prices

Which of the numbers above can be approximated? Which need to be given exactly?

You should have an idea if the answer to a calculation is about the right size or not. There are some ways of checking answers. First, when it is a multiplication, you can check that the final digit is correct. Second, you can round numbers off and do a mental calculation to see if an answer is about the right size. Third, you can check by doing the inverse operation.

Example 2.8 ▶ Explain why these calculations must be wrong.

   a $23 \times 45 = 1053$ **b** $19 \times 59 = 121$

   a The last digit should be 5, because the product of the last digits is 15. That is, $23 \times 45 = \dots5$

   b The answer is roughly $20 \times 60 = 1200$.

Example 2.9 ▶ Estimate answers to these calculations.

   a $\dfrac{21.3 + 48.7}{6.4}$ **b** 31.2×48.5 **c** $359 \div 42$

   a Round off the numbers on the top to $20 + 50 = 70$. Round off 6.4 to 7. Then $70 \div 7 = 10$.

   b Round off to 30×50, which is $3 \times 5 \times 100 = 1500$.

   c Round off to $360 \div 40$, which is $36 \div 4 = 9$.

Example 2.10 ▶ By using the inverse operation, check if each calculation is correct.

   a $450 \div 6 = 75$ **b** $310 - 59 = 249$

   a By the inverse operation, $450 = 6 \times 75$. This is true and can be checked mentally: $6 \times 70 = 420$, $6 \times 5 = 30$, $420 + 30 = 450$.

   b By the inverse operation, $310 = 249 + 59$. This must end in 8 as $9 + 9 = 18$, so it cannot be correct.

Exercise 2D

1 Explain why these calculations must be wrong.

   a $24 \times 42 = 1080$ **b** $51 \times 73 = 723$ **c** $\dfrac{34.5 + 63.2}{9.7} = 20.07$

   d $360 \div 8 = 35$ **e** $354 - 37 = 323$

2 Estimate the answer to each of these problems.

a $2768 - 392$ b 231×18 c $792 \div 38$ d $\dfrac{36.7 + 23.2}{14.1}$

e 423×423 f $157.2 \div 38.2$ g $\dfrac{135.7 - 68.2}{15.8 - 8.9}$ h $\dfrac{38.9 \times 61.2}{39.6 - 18.4}$

3 Delroy had £10. In his shopping basket he had a magazine costing £2.65, some batteries costing £1.92, and a tape costing £4.99. Without adding up the numbers, how could Delroy be sure he had enough to buy the goods in the basket? Explain a quick way for Delroy to find out if he could afford a 45p bar of chocolate as well.

4 Amy bought 6 bottles of pop at 46p per bottle. The shopkeeper asked her for £3.16. Without working out the correct answer, explain why this is wrong.

5 A first class stamp is 27p. I need eight. Will £2 be enough to pay for them? Explain your answer clearly.

6 In a shop I bought a 53p comic and a £1.47 model car. The till said £54.47. Why?

7 Which is the best approximation for $50.7 - 39.2$?

a $506 - 392$ b $51 - 39$ c $50 - 39$ d $5.06 - 3.92$

8 Which is the best approximation for 19.3×42.6?

a 20×40 b 19×42 c 19×40 d 20×42

9 Which is the best estimate for $54.6 \div 10.9$?

a $500 \div 100$ b $54 \div 11$ c $50 \div 11$ d $55 \div 11$

10 Estimate the number the arrow is pointing to.

a
18   20

b
−2   8

c
−1.2   0.8

Extension Work

The first 15 **square numbers** are 1, 4, 9, 16, 25, 36, 49, 64, 81, 100, 121, 144, 169, 196 and 225. The inverse operation of squaring a number is to find its **square root**. So $\sqrt{121} = 11$. Only the square numbers have integer square roots. Other square roots have to be estimated or found from a calculator.

For example, to find the square root of 30 use a diagram like that on the right, to estimate that $\sqrt{30} \approx 5.48$. (A check shows that $5.48^2 = 30.03$.)

Here is another example. Find $\sqrt{45}$.

The diagram shows that $\sqrt{45} \approx 6.7$. (Check: $6.7^2 = 44.89$)

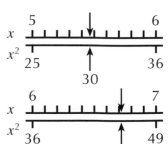

Use the above method to find $\sqrt{20}$, $\sqrt{55}$, $\sqrt{75}$, $\sqrt{110}$, $\sqrt{140}$, $\sqrt{200}$. Check your answers with a calculator.

Column method for addition and subtraction

Look at the picture. What is wrong?

You may have several ways of adding and subtracting numbers, such as estimation or using a number line. Here you will be shown how to set out additions and subtractions using the column method. You may already have learnt about 'lining up the units digit'. This is not strictly correct. What you do is 'line up the decimal points'.

Example 2.11 ▶

Work out, without using a calculator: **a** $3.27 + 14.8$ **b** $12.8 - 3.45$

a   Write the numbers in columns, lining up the decimal points. You should fill the gap with a zero.

$$
\begin{array}{r}
3.27 \\
+\ 14.80 \\
\hline
18.07 \\
{\scriptstyle 1}
\end{array}
$$

Note the carry digit in the units column, because $2 + 8 = 10$.

b   Write the numbers in columns and fill the gap with a zero.

$$
\begin{array}{r}
{\scriptstyle 0\ 1\ 7\ 1} \\
12.80 \\
-\ 3.45 \\
\hline
9.35
\end{array}
$$

Note that, because you cannot take 5 from 0, you have to borrow from the next column. This means that 8 becomes 7 and zero becomes 10.

Example 2.12 ▶

Work out $3.14 + 14.5 - 8.72$.

This type of problem needs to be done in two stages. First, do the addition and then do the subtraction.

$$
\begin{array}{r}
3.14 \\
+\ 14.50 \\
\hline
17.64
\end{array}
\qquad
\begin{array}{r}
{\scriptstyle 0\ 16\ 1} \\
17.64 \\
-\ 8.72 \\
\hline
8.92
\end{array}
$$

1 By means of a drawing, show how you would use a number line to work out the answers to these.

    a 2.4 + 3.7   **b** 5.3 + 7.45   **c** 8.4 – 5.6   **d** 9.4 – 4.86

2 Repeat the calculations in Question 1 using the column method. Show all your working.

3 Use the column method to work out the following additions.

    a 37.1 + 14.2   **b** 32.6 + 15.73   **c** 6.78 + 4.59   **d** 9.62 + 0.7

    e 4.79 + 1.2   **f** 6.08 + 2.16   **g** 1.2 + 3.41 + 4.56

    h 76.57 + 312.5 + 6.08

4 Use the column method to work out the following subtractions.

    a 37.1 – 14.2   **b** 32.6 – 15.73   **c** 6.78 – 4.59   **d** 9.62 – 0.7

    e 4.79 – 1.2   **f** 6.08 – 2.16   **g** 1.2 + 3.41 – 4.56

    h 76.57 + 312.5 – 6.08

Extension Work

$6 \times 8 = 48$ $6 \times 0.8 = 4.8$ $0.6 \times 0.8 = 0.48$

When these calculations are set out in columns, they look like this:

$$
\begin{array}{r} 8 \\ \times\ 6 \\ \hline 48 \end{array}
\qquad
\begin{array}{r} 0.8 \\ \times\ 6.0 \\ \hline 4.8 \end{array}
\qquad
\begin{array}{r} 0.8 \\ \times\ 0.6 \\ \hline 0.48 \end{array}
$$

The column method does not work when we multiply decimals.

Use a calculator to find out the rules for where the decimal point goes in multiplication problems such as

    3×0.2 5×0.7 0.3×0.9 0.2×0.6 0.03×0.5

Solving problems

A bus starts at Barnsley and makes four stops before reaching Penistone. At Barnsley 23 people get on. At Dodworth 12 people get off and 14 people get on. At Silkstone 15 people get off and 4 people get on. At Hoylandswaine 5 people get off and 6 people get on. At Cubley 9 people get off and 8 get on. At Penistone the rest of the passengers get off. How many people are on the bus?

When you solve problems, you need to develop a strategy: that is, a way to go about the problem. You also have to decide which mathematical operation you need to solve it. For example, is it addition, subtraction, multiplication or division or a combination of these? Something else you must do is to read the question fully before starting. The answer to the problem above is one! The driver.

Read the questions below carefully.

1 It cost six people £15 to go to the cinema. How much would it cost eight people?

2 Ten pencils cost £4.50. How much would seven pencils cost?

3 A water tank holds 500 litres. How much has been used if there is 143.7 litres left in the tank?

4 Strips of paper are 40 cm long. They are stuck together with a 10 cm overlap.

a How long would two strips glued together be?
b How long would four strips glued together be?

5 A can of coke and a Kit-Kat together cost 80p. Two cans of coke and a Kit-Kat together cost £1.30. How much would three cans of coke and four Kit-Kats cost?

6 To make a number chain, start with any number.

When the number is even, divide it by 2.

When the number is odd, multiply it by 3 and add 1.

If you start with 13, the chain becomes 13, 40, 20, 10, 5, 16, 8, 4, 2, 1, 4, 2, 1, …

The chain repeats 4, 2, 1, 4, 2, 1. So, stop the chain when it gets to 1.

Start with other numbers below 20. What is the longest chain you can make before you get to 1?

7 If $135 \times 44 = 5940$, write down, without calculating, the value of:

a 13.5×4.4 **b** 1.35×44 **c** 1.35×4.4 **d** 1350×440

8 Find four consecutive odd numbers that add up to 80.

9 30 can be worked out as $33 - 3$. Can you find two other ways of working out 30 using three equal digits?

10 Arrange the numbers 1, 2, 3 and 4 in each of these to make the problem correct.

a $\square + \square = \square + \square$ **b** $\square \times \square = \square\square$ **c** $\square\square \div \square = \square$

Extension Work

Using the numbers 1, 2, 3 and 4 and any mathematical signs, make all of the numbers from 1 to 10.

For example: $2 \times 3 - 4 - 1 = 1$, $12 - 3 - 4 = 5$

Once you have found all the numbers up to 10, can you find totals above 10?

What you need to know for level 4

- Addition and subtraction facts up to 20 + 20
- Multiplication tables up to 10 × 10
- The place value of whole numbers
- How to multiply and divide whole numbers by 10 and 100
- How to add and subtract decimals with up to two decimal places

What you need to know for level 5

- How to estimate answers and check if an answer is about right
- How to multiply and divide decimals by 10, 100 and 1000
- How to add and subtract using negative and positive numbers
- How to solve problems using a variety of mathematical methods

National Curriculum SATs questions

LEVEL 4

1 *1997 Paper 1*

  a Fill in the missing numbers so that the answer is always 45.

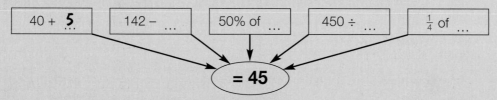

  b Fill in the gaps below to make the answer 45.

  You may use any of these signs: + − × ÷

  28 … 2 … 31 = 45

2 *1997 Paper 1*

  a Look at this part of a number line. Fill in the two missing numbers.

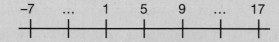

  Finish this sentence: The numbers on this number line go up in steps of ……

  b This is a different number line. Fill in the three missing numbers

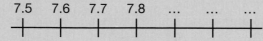

  Finish this sentence: The numbers on this number line go up in steps of ……

3   *1999 Paper 1*

Write one number at the end of each question to make it correct.

a   38 + 17 = 28 + ...

b   38 − 17 = 28 − ...

c   40 × 10 = 4 × ...

d   7000 ÷ 10 = 700 ÷ ...

```
1 × 65 = 65
2 × 65 = 130
3 × 65 = 195
4 × 65 = 260
5 × 65 = 325
6 × 65 = 390
7 × 65 = 455
8 × 65 = 520
9 × 65 = 585
10 × 65 = 650
```

4   *2000 Paper 1*

Here is the 65 times table.

Use the 65 times table to help you work out 16 × 65.

Show how you did it.

5   *2001 Paper 1*

a   In New York the temperature was −2 °C. In Atlanta the temperature was 7 °C warmer. What was the temperature in Atlanta?

b   In Amsterdam the temperature was 3 °C. In Helsinki the temperature was −8 °C. How many degrees warmer was it in Amsterdam than in Helsinki?

LEVEL 5

6   *1997 Paper 2*

Look at these number cards.   +3 0 −5 +9 +2 −8 +7 −2

a   Choose a card to give the answer

 + + ☐ = 4

b   Choose a card to give the lowest possible answer.
Work out the answer.

 + ☐ = ...

c   Choose a card to give the lowest possible answer.
Work out the answer.

−2 − ☐ = ...

d   Now choose a card to give the highest possible answer.
Work out the answer.

−2 − ☐ = ...

7   *1999 Paper 1*

Here is a list of numbers: −7   −5   −3   −1   0   2   4   6

a   What is the total of all eight of the numbers on the list?

b   Choose the three numbers from the list which have the lowest possible total.

Write the numbers and their total. You must not use the same number more than once.

... + ... + ... = ...

CHAPTER 3

Shape, Space and Measures **1**

This chapter is going to show you

- how to estimate and calculate perimeters and areas of 2-D shapes
- how to calculate the area of a rectangle
- how to draw 3-D shapes and how to calculate the surface area of a cuboid

What you should already know

- How to measure and draw lines
- How to find the perimeter of a shape
- Area is measured in square centimetres
- How to draw the net of a cube
- The names of 3-D shapes such as the cube and cuboid

Length, perimeter and area

The metric units of length in common use are: the millimetre (mm)
the centimetre (cm)
the metre (m)
the kilometre (km)

The metric units of area in common use are: the square millimetre (mm^2)
the square centimetre (cm^2)
the square metre (m^2)
the square kilometre (km^2)

Example 3.1

The length of this line is 72 mm or 7.2 cm.

Example 3.2

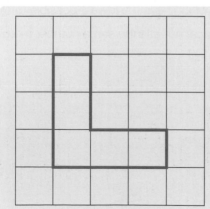

The side of each square on the grid represents 1 cm.

The perimeter of the L-shape = 1 + 2 + 2 + 1 + 3 + 3
= 12 cm

By counting the squares, the area of the L-shape = 5 cm^2

Example 3.3 ▶

Estimate the area of the shape.

Each square on the grid has an area of 1 cm².

Mark each square which is at least half a square with a dot.

There are 11 dotted squares. So, an estimate for the area of the shape is 11 cm².

Exercise 3A

1 Measure the length of each of the following lines. Give your answer in centimetres.

a ──────────

b ───────────

c ────────────

d ────────────

e ──────────────────

2 Find the perimeter of each of these shapes by using your ruler to measure the length of each side.

a b c d

3 Copy these shapes onto 1 cm squared paper. Find the perimeter and area of each shape.

a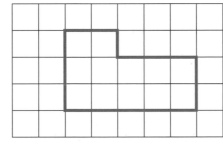

b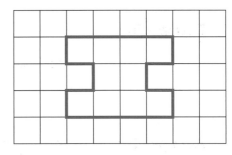

c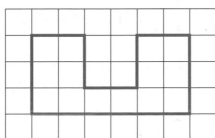

d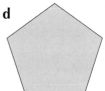

4 Estimate the area of each of these shapes. Each square on the grid represents one square centimetre.

a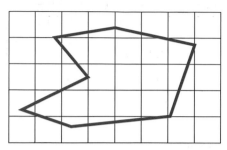

b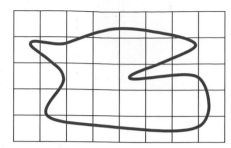

Extension Work

Working in groups, draw the outline of each person's hand (or foot) on 1 cm squared paper. Estimate the area of each hand (or foot).

Make a display of all the hands (and/or feet) for your classroom.

Perimeter and area of rectangles

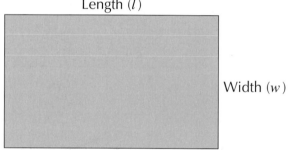

Length (l)

Width (w)

The perimeter of a rectangle is the total distance around the shape.

Perimeter = 2 lengths + 2 widths

$$P = 2l + 2w$$ Unit is mm, cm or m.

The area of the rectangle is the amount of space inside the shape.

Area = Length × Width

$$A = l \times w \text{ or } A = lw$$ Unit is mm², cm² or m².

Example 3.4 ▷ Find the perimeter and area of each of the following.

a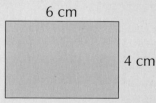
6 cm

4 cm

$P = 2 \times 6 + 2 \times 4$
$= 12 + 8$
$= 20$ cm

$A = 6 \times 4$
$= 24$ cm²

b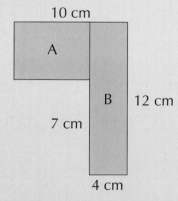
10 cm

A

B   12 cm

7 cm

4 cm

$P = 10 + 12 + 4 + 7 + 6 + 5$
$= 44$ cm

Total area = Area of A + Area of B
$= 6 \times 5 + 12 \times 4$
$= 30 + 48$
$= 78$ cm²

1 Find the perimeter of each rectangle.

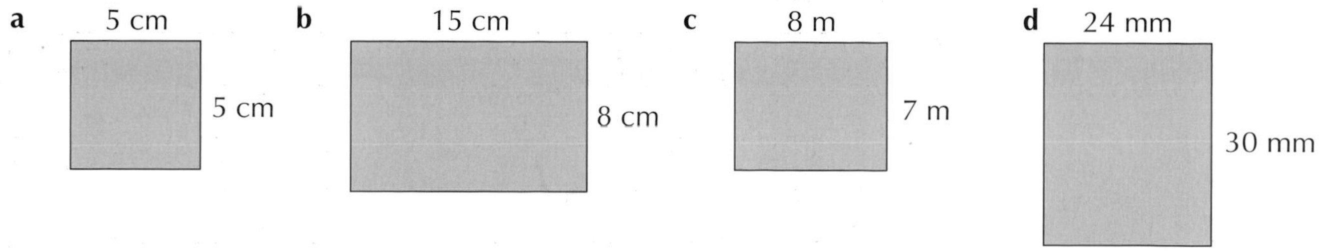

a 5 cm
5 cm

b 15 cm
8 cm

c 8 m
7 m

d 24 mm
30 mm

2 a Find the perimeter of this room.

b Skirting board is sold in 3 m lengths. How many lengths are needed to go around the four walls of the room?

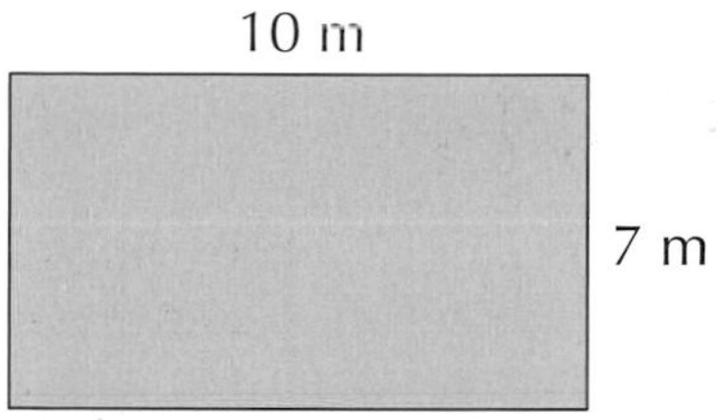

10 m
7 m

3 A paving slab measures 0.8 m by 0.6 m. Find the perimeter of the slab.

4 Find the area of each rectangle.

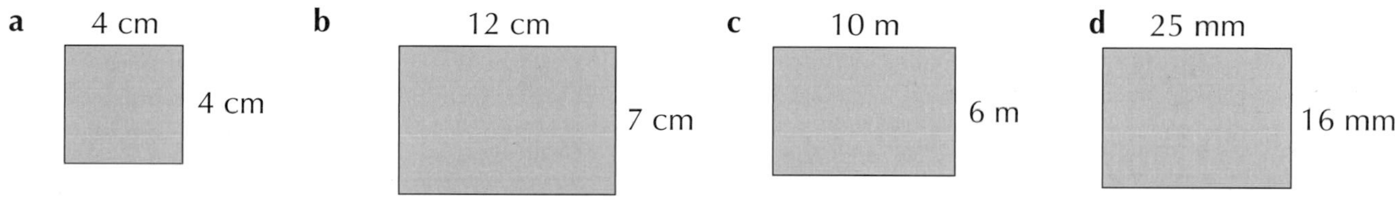

a 4 cm
4 cm

b 12 cm
7 cm

c 10 m
6 m

d 25 mm
16 mm

5 A room measures 6 m by 4 m.

a What is the area of the floor?

b The floor is to be covered using square carpet tiles measuring 50 cm by 50 cm. How many tiles are needed to cover the floor?

6 Calculate the perimeter of this square.   25 cm²

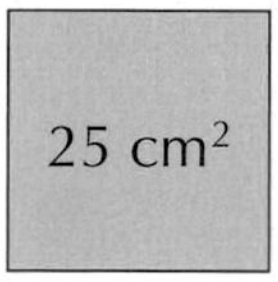

7 Copy and complete the table for rectangles **a** to **f**.

	Length	Width	Perimeter	Area
a	8 cm	6 cm		
b	20 cm	15 cm		
c	10 cm		30 cm	
d		5 m	22 m	
e	7 m			42 m²
f		10 mm		250 mm²

8 Find **i** the perimeter and **ii** the area of each of the following compound shapes.

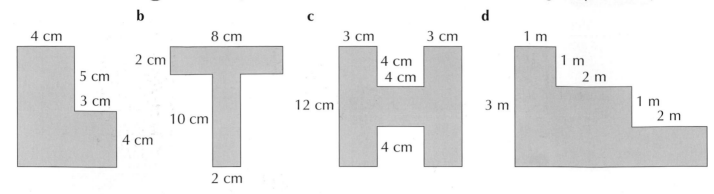

a
4 cm
5 cm
3 cm
4 cm

b
8 cm
2 cm
10 cm
2 cm

c
3 cm   3 cm
4 cm
4 cm
12 cm
4 cm

d
1 m
1 m
2 m
3 m
1 m
2 m

9 Phil finds the area of this compound shape.

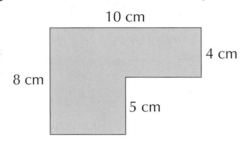

10 cm
4 cm
8 cm
5 cm

This is his working:

Area = 10 x 4 + 8 x 5
= 40 + 40
= 80 cm²

a Explain why he is wrong.

b Calculate the correct answer.

10 Sandra makes a picture frame from a rectangular piece of card for a photograph of her favourite group.

a Find the area of the photograph.

b Find the area of the card she uses.

c Find the area of the border.

20 cm   14 cm
24 cm
30 cm

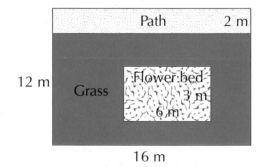

Path   2 m
12 m   Grass
Flower bed
3 m
6 m
16 m

11 A garden is in the shape of a rectangle measuring 16 m by 12 m.

Calculate the area of the grass in the garden.

12 How many rectangles can you draw with a fixed perimeter of 20 cm but each one having a different area?

Extension Work

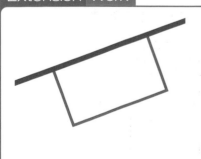

1 Sheep pens

A farmer has 60 m of fence to make a rectangular sheep pen against a wall. Find the length and width of the pen in order to make its area as large as possible.

2 Squares on a chessboard

How many squares on a chessboard?

3-D shapes

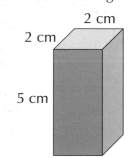

You should be able to recognise and name the following 3-D shapes or solids.

Cube   Cuboid   Pyramid Tetrahedron Triangular prism Cone   Cylinder   Sphere   Hemisphere

Some of these solids can be drawn in several ways, as Example 3.5 shows.

Example 3.5 ▷

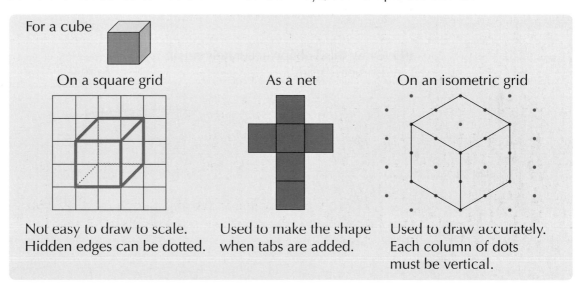

For a cube

On a square grid

Not easy to draw to scale. Hidden edges can be dotted.

As a net

Used to make the shape when tabs are added.

On an isometric grid

Used to draw accurately. Each column of dots must be vertical.

Exercise 3C

1 On squared paper, draw accurate nets for each of the following cuboids.

a
4 cm
3 cm
2 cm

b
2 cm
2 cm
5 cm

2 A cuboid has six faces, eight vertices and 12 edges.

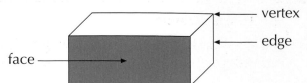

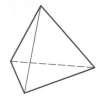

How many faces, vertices and edges do each of the following 3-D shapes have?

a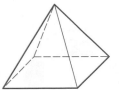

b

c

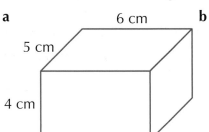

Square-based pyramid   Triangular prism   Tetrahedron

3 Draw each of the following cuboids accurately on an isometric grid.

a 6 cm 5 cm 4 cm

b 2 cm 2 cm 5 cm

c 5 cm 2 cm 1 cm

4 Draw this T-shape accurately on an isometric grid.

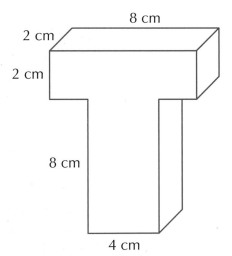

2 cm 8 cm 2 cm 8 cm 4 cm

5 How many cubes are required to make this solid?

Draw other similar solids of your own on an isometric grid.

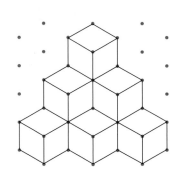

1 Euler's theorem

Copy and complete the following table for seven different polyhedrons.
Ask your teacher to show you these 3-D shapes.

Solid	Number of faces	Number of vertices	Number of edges
Cuboid			
Square-based pyramid			
Triangular prism			
Tetrahedron			
Hexagonal prism			
Octahedron			
Dodecahedron			

Find a formula that connects the number of faces, vertices and edges.

This formula is named after Léonard Euler, a famous eighteenth-century Swiss mathematician.

2 Pentominoes

A pentomino is a 2-D shape made from five squares that touch side to side.
Here are two examples.

 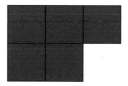

a Draw on squared paper as many different pentominoes as you can.

b How many of these pentominoes are nets that make an open cube?

3 Four cubes

On an isometric grid, draw all the possible different solids that can be made from four cubes. Here is an example.

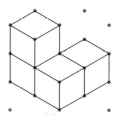

Surface area of cubes and cuboids

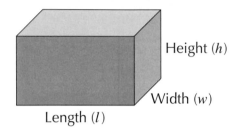

Height (h)

Width (w)

Length (l)

The surface area of a cuboid is found by calculating the total area of its six faces.

Area of top and bottom faces = 2 × length × width = $2lw$

Area of front and back faces = 2 × length × height = $2lh$

Area of the two sides = 2 × width × height = $2wh$

Surface area of cuboid = $S = 2lw + 2lh + 2wh$

Example 3.6

Find the surface area of this cuboid.

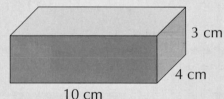

3 cm

4 cm

10 cm

$$S = (2 \times 10 \times 4) + (2 \times 10 \times 3) + (2 \times 4 \times 3)$$
$$= 80 + 60 + 24$$
$$= 164 \text{ cm}^2$$

Exercise 3D

1 Find the surface area for each of the following cuboids.

a

10 cm

5 cm

6 cm

b

3 cm

12 cm

2 cm

c

5 cm

4 cm

15 cm

d

2 cm

3 cm

8 cm

2 Find the surface area of this unit cube.

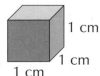

1 cm

1 cm

1 cm

3 Find the surface area for each of the cubes with the following edge lengths.

    a   2 cm   **b**   5 cm   **c**   10 cm   **d**   8 m

4 Find the surface area of the cereal packet on the left.

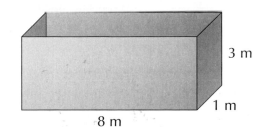

5 Find the surface area of the outside of this open water tank.
(A cuboid without a top.)

3 m

8 m

1 m

6 Find the total surface area of this 3-D shape.

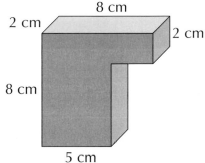

8 cm

2 cm

2 cm

8 cm

5 cm

7 Six unit (centimetre) cubes are placed together to make the following 3-D shapes.

a

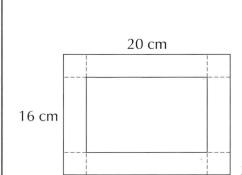

b

c

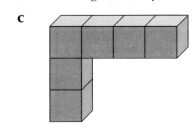

Find the surface area of each shape.

Extension Work

1 Estimating

Estimate the surface area for various everyday objects in the shape of cuboids.

Check your estimate by measuring.

2 Open box problem

20 cm

16 cm

An open box is made from a piece of card, measuring 20 cm by 16 cm, by cutting off a square from each corner.

Investigate the surface area of the open box formed for different sizes of square cut off.

You may wish to put your data on a computer spreadsheet.

3 Cubes to cuboids.

Twenty unit cubes are arranged to form a cuboid.

How many different cuboids can you make?

Which one has the greatest surface area?

What you need to know for level 4

- How to draw and measure straight lines
- How to draw common 2-D shapes
- How to find the perimeter of a 2-D shape
- How to find the area of a 2-D shape by counting squares

What you need to know for level 5

- How to calculate the area of a rectangle by using the formula $A = lw$
- How to draw nets for 3-D shapes
- How to draw 3-D shapes on an isometric grid
- How to calculate the surface area of a cuboid

National Curriculum SATs questions

LEVEL 4

1 *2000 Paper 2*

The shaded rectangle has an area of 4 cm² and a perimeter of 10 cm.

a Look at the cross-shape.

The cross-shape has an area of ... cm² and a perimeter of ... cm.

b Draw a shape with an area of 6 cm²

c What is the perimeter of your shape?

2 *2001 Paper 2*

Alika has a box of square tiles.

The tiles are three different sizes.

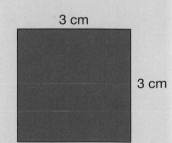

1 cm
1 cm
1 by 1 tile

2 cm
2 cm
2 by 2 tile

3 cm
3 cm
3 by 3 tile

She also has a mat that is 6 cm by 6 cm.

36 of the 1 by 1 tiles will cover the mat.

a How many of the 2 by 2 tiles will cover the mat?

b How many of the 3 by 3 tiles will cover the mat?

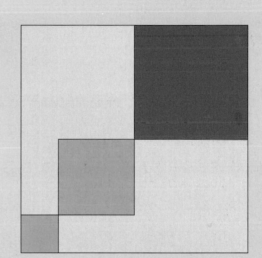

6 cm

6 cm

c Alika glues three tiles on her mat like this. Complete the gaps below.

She could cover the rest of the mat by using another two 3 by 3 tiles and another ... 1 by 1 tiles.

She could cover the rest of the mat by using another two 2 by 2 tiles and another ... 1 by 1 tiles.

LEVEL 5

3 *1999 Paper 1*

The diagram shows a rectangle 18 cm long and 14 cm wide.

It has been split into four smaller rectangles.

Write the area of each small rectangle on a sketch of the diagram.

One has been done for you.

What is the area of the whole rectangle?

What is 18×14?

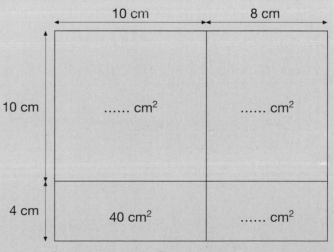

10 cm   8 cm

10 cm   ...... cm²   ...... cm²

4 cm   40 cm²   ...... cm²

4 *2000 Paper 2*

I make a model with 6 cubes.

The drawings show my model from different views.

View A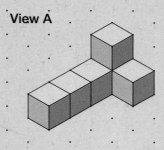

View B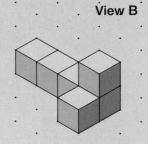

a I join one more cube to my model.

The drawing from view A shows where I join the cube.

Complete the drawing from view B.

View A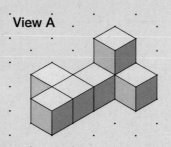

View B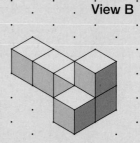

b Then I move the cube to a different position.

Complete the drawing from view B.

View A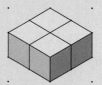

View B

5 *1999 Paper 2*

This cuboid is made from 4 small cubes

a Draw a cuboid which is twice as high, twice as long and twice as wide.

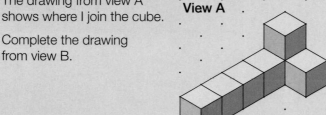

b Graham made this cuboid from 3 small cubes.

Mohinder wants to make a cuboid which is twice as high, twice as long and twice as wide as Graham's cuboid.

How many small cubes will Mohinder need altogether?

CHAPTER 4 Number 2

This chapter is going to show you:

- how to extend your knowledge of fractions and percentages
- how to add simple fractions
- how to find equivalent fractions, percentages and decimals

What you should already know

- How to change an improper fraction into a mixed number
- How to use decimal notation for tenths and hundredths
- How to recognise simple equivalent fractions

Fractions

These diagrams show you five ways to split a 4 by 4 grid into quarters.

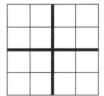 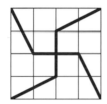 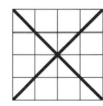 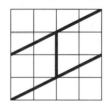 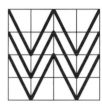

How many more different ways can you find to do this?

What about splitting the 4 by 4 grid into halves?

Example 4.1 ▶ Write down the fraction of each shape that is shaded.

a 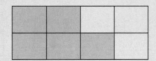   b 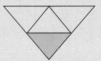   c

a $\frac{5}{8}$ The shape is divided into 8 equal parts (the denominator) and 5 parts are shaded (the numerator).

b $\frac{1}{4}$ The shape is divided into 4 equal parts (the denominator) and 1 part is shaded (the numerator).

c $\frac{5}{6}$ The shape is divided into 6 equal parts (the denominator) and 5 parts are shaded (the numerator).

Example 4.2 ▶ Fill in the missing number in each of these equivalent fractions.

a $\dfrac{1}{3} = \dfrac{\square}{15}$ **b** $\dfrac{5}{8} = \dfrac{\square}{32}$ **c** $\dfrac{15}{27} = \dfrac{5}{\square}$

a   Multiply by 5   **b**   Multiply by 4   **c**   Divide by 3

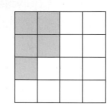 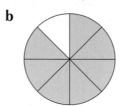 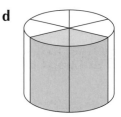

Exercise 4A

1 Write down the fraction of each shape that is shaded.

a   **b**   **c**   **d**

2 Draw a fraction diagram and shade it to show each fraction.

a $\dfrac{1}{4}$ **b** $\dfrac{2}{5}$ **c** $\dfrac{3}{8}$ **d** $\dfrac{1}{7}$

3 Copy and complete the following equivalent fraction series.

a $\dfrac{1}{2} = \dfrac{2}{\ldots} = \dfrac{\ldots}{6} = \dfrac{8}{\ldots} = \dfrac{\ldots}{20} = \dfrac{\ldots}{150}$

b $\dfrac{3}{4} = \dfrac{6}{\ldots} = \dfrac{\ldots}{12} = \dfrac{12}{\ldots} = \dfrac{\ldots}{40} = \dfrac{\ldots}{160}$

4 Find the missing number in each of these equivalent fractions.

a $\dfrac{2}{3} = \dfrac{\square}{9}$ **b** $\dfrac{3}{8} = \dfrac{\square}{16}$ **c** $\dfrac{5}{9} = \dfrac{\square}{27}$

d $\dfrac{2}{5} = \dfrac{\square}{15}$ **e** $\dfrac{3}{7} = \dfrac{\square}{28}$ **f** $\dfrac{4}{9} = \dfrac{\square}{36}$

g $\dfrac{1}{5} = \dfrac{\square}{25}$ **h** $\dfrac{2}{11} = \dfrac{14}{\square}$ **i** $\dfrac{4}{9} = \dfrac{20}{\square}$

5 Cancel each of these fractions to its simplest form.

a $\dfrac{4}{12}$ **b** $\dfrac{6}{9}$ **c** $\dfrac{14}{21}$ **d** $\dfrac{15}{20}$ **e** $\dfrac{18}{20}$ **f** $\dfrac{20}{50}$

g $\dfrac{8}{24}$ **h** $\dfrac{6}{12}$ **i** $\dfrac{4}{24}$ **j** $\dfrac{12}{20}$ **k** $\dfrac{16}{24}$ **l** $\dfrac{25}{35}$

m $\dfrac{6}{14}$ **n** $\dfrac{12}{9}$ **o** $\dfrac{18}{27}$ **p** $\dfrac{45}{20}$ **q** $\dfrac{28}{10}$ **r** $\dfrac{120}{40}$

6 Clocks have 12 divisions around the face. What fraction of a full turn does

a   the minute hand turn through from 7:15 to 7:35?

b   the minute hand turn through from 8:25 to 9:25?

c   the hour hand turn through from 1:00 to 4:00?

d   the hour hand turn through from 4:00 to 5:30?

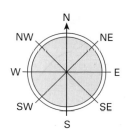

7 This compass rose has eight divisions around its face. What fraction of a turn takes you from

  a NW to SW clockwise?   **b** E to S anticlockwise?

  c NE to S clockwise?   **d** S to NE anticlockwise?

  e W to SE clockwise?   **f** N to NW clockwise?

8 Give each answer in its lowest terms.

  a 1 metre is 100 cm. What fraction of a metre is 35 cm?

  b 1 kilogram is 1000 grams. What fraction of a kilogram is 550 grams?

  c 1 hour is 60 minutes. What fraction of 1 hour is 33 minutes?

  d 1 kilometres is 1000 metres. What fraction of a kilometre is 75 metres?

Extension Work

There are 360° in one full turn. 90° is $\frac{90°}{360°} = \frac{1}{4}$ of a full turn.

1 What fraction of a full turn is each of these?

  a 60°   **b** 20°   **c** 180°   **d** 30°

  e 45°   **f** 36°   **g** 5°   **h** 450°

2 How many degrees is   **a** $\frac{1}{8}$ of a full turn?   **b** $\frac{1}{5}$ of a full turn?

3 360 was the number of days in a year according to the Ancient Egyptians. They also thought that numbers with lots of factors had magical properties. Find all the factors of 360.

4 Explain how the factors can be used to work out what fraction of a full turn is 40°.

Fractions and decimals

All of the grids below contain 100 squares. Some of the squares have been shaded in. In each case, write down the amount that has been shaded as a fraction, a percentage and a decimal. What connections can you see between the equivalent values?

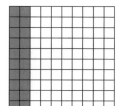 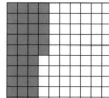 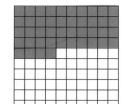 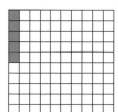 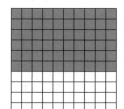 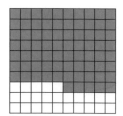

Example 4.3 Convert each of the following decimals to a fraction: **a** 0.65   **b** 0.44

  a $0.65 = \frac{65}{100} = \frac{13}{20}$ (cancel by 5)   **b** $0.44 = \frac{44}{100} = \frac{11}{25}$ (cancel by 4)

Example 4.4 ▶

Convert each of the following fractions to a decimal: **a** $\frac{12}{25}$ **b** $\frac{7}{8}$

a Multiply top and bottom by 4: $\frac{12}{25}\frac{(\times 4)}{(\times 4)} = \frac{48}{100} = 0.48$

b Multiply top and bottom by 12.5: $\frac{7}{8}\frac{(\times 12.5)}{(\times 12.5)} = \frac{87.5}{100} = 0.875$

Example 4.5 ▶

Put the correct sign, < or >, between each pair of fractions **a** $\frac{5}{8} \ldots \frac{3}{5}$ **b** $\frac{16}{25} \ldots \frac{7}{10}$

a Convert to fractions out of 100 (or decimals):

$\frac{5}{8} = \frac{62.5}{100} = 0.625, \frac{3}{5} = \frac{60}{100} = 0.6$, so $\frac{5}{8} > \frac{3}{5}$

b Convert to fractions out of 100 (or decimals):

$\frac{16}{25} = \frac{64}{100} = 0.64, \frac{7}{10} = \frac{70}{100} = 0.7$, so $\frac{16}{25} < \frac{7}{10}$

Exercise 4B

1 Convert each of these top-heavy fractions to a mixed number.

a $\frac{3}{2}$ **b** $\frac{7}{5}$ **c** $\frac{9}{7}$ **d** $\frac{17}{8}$ **e** $\frac{15}{2}$ **f** $\frac{22}{7}$

g $\frac{32}{15}$ **h** $\frac{17}{5}$ **i** $\frac{12}{5}$ **j** $\frac{13}{6}$ **k** $\frac{9}{4}$ **l** $\frac{41}{10}$

2 Convert each of these mixed numbers to a top-heavy fraction.

a $1\frac{1}{4}$ **b** $2\frac{1}{2}$ **c** $3\frac{1}{6}$ **d** $4\frac{2}{7}$ **e** $5\frac{1}{8}$ **f** $2\frac{3}{5}$

g $1\frac{7}{8}$ **h** $3\frac{3}{4}$ **i** $3\frac{2}{5}$ **j** $2\frac{3}{11}$ **k** $4\frac{5}{8}$ **l** $3\frac{2}{9}$

3 Convert each of the following decimals to a fraction.

a 0.2 **b** 0.28 **c** 0.35 **d** 0.85 **e** 0.9 **f** 0.16

g 0.24 **h** 0.48 **i** 0.95 **j** 0.05 **k** 0.99 **l** 0.27

4 Convert each of the following fractions to a decimal.

a $\frac{3}{10}$ **b** $\frac{4}{25}$ **c** $\frac{3}{20}$ **d** $\frac{3}{8}$ **e** $\frac{23}{100}$ **f** $\frac{6}{25}$

g $\frac{7}{50}$ **h** $\frac{14}{25}$ **i** $\frac{13}{20}$ **j** $\frac{11}{10}$ **k** $\frac{115}{50}$ **l** $\frac{26}{25}$

5 Put the correct sign, < or >, between each pair of fractions.

a $\frac{7}{50} \ldots \frac{2}{20}$ **b** $\frac{27}{50} \ldots \frac{13}{25}$ **c** $\frac{9}{10} \ldots \frac{22}{25}$

6 Put each set of fractions in order of size, smallest first.

a $\frac{7}{25}, \frac{3}{10}, \frac{1}{4}$ **b** $\frac{3}{4}, \frac{37}{50}, \frac{7}{10}$ **c** $1\frac{6}{25}, 1\frac{1}{4}, 1\frac{11}{50}$

7 Which of these fractions is nearer to 1: $\frac{5}{8}$ or $\frac{8}{5}$? Show all your working.

$\frac{1}{8}$	$\frac{2}{8}$	$\frac{3}{8}$					
$\frac{1}{7}$							
$\frac{1}{6}$			$\frac{4}{6}$				
$\frac{1}{5}$		$\frac{2}{5}$					
$\frac{1}{4}$		$\frac{2}{4}$					
$\frac{1}{3}$			$\frac{2}{3}$		$\frac{3}{3}$		
$\frac{1}{2}$			$\frac{2}{2}$				
1							

On squared paper outline an 8 × 8 grid.

Mark it off as shown. Then fill in the rest of the values in the boxes.

Use the diagram to put the correct sign (<, > or =) between each pair of fractions.

a $\frac{2}{7} \ldots \frac{1}{5}$ **b** $\frac{3}{8} \ldots \frac{1}{3}$ **c** $\frac{3}{4} \ldots \frac{6}{8}$

d $\frac{1}{2} \ldots \frac{4}{7}$ **e** $\frac{2}{8} \ldots \frac{1}{4}$ **f** $\frac{3}{7} \ldots \frac{1}{3}$

g $\frac{3}{5} \ldots \frac{2}{3}$ **h** $\frac{1}{2} \ldots \frac{5}{8}$ **i** $\frac{5}{8} \ldots \frac{3}{5}$

j $\frac{3}{6} \ldots \frac{1}{2}$ **k** $\frac{5}{7} \ldots \frac{3}{4}$ **l** $\frac{2}{3} \ldots \frac{4}{6}$

Adding and subtracting fractions

Look at the fraction chart and the number line. Explain how you could use the line to show that

$$1\frac{1}{2} + \frac{7}{8} = 2\frac{3}{8} \quad \text{and} \quad 1\frac{1}{2} - \frac{7}{8} = \frac{5}{8}.$$

$\frac{1}{8}$	$\frac{1}{4}$	$\frac{3}{8}$	$\frac{1}{2}$	$\frac{5}{8}$	$\frac{3}{4}$	$\frac{7}{8}$	1
$1\frac{1}{8}$	$1\frac{1}{4}$	$1\frac{3}{8}$	$1\frac{1}{2}$	$1\frac{5}{8}$	$1\frac{3}{4}$	$1\frac{7}{8}$	2
$2\frac{1}{8}$	$2\frac{1}{4}$	$2\frac{3}{8}$	$2\frac{1}{2}$	$2\frac{5}{8}$	$2\frac{3}{4}$	$2\frac{7}{8}$	3
$3\frac{1}{8}$	$3\frac{1}{4}$	$3\frac{3}{8}$	$3\frac{1}{2}$	$3\frac{5}{8}$	$3\frac{3}{4}$	$3\frac{7}{8}$	4

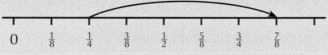

0 $\frac{1}{8}$ $\frac{1}{4}$ $\frac{3}{8}$ $\frac{1}{2}$ $\frac{5}{8}$ $\frac{3}{4}$ $\frac{7}{8}$ 1 $1\frac{1}{8}$ $1\frac{1}{4}$ $1\frac{3}{8}$ $1\frac{1}{2}$

Example 4.6

Add the following fractions: **a** $2\frac{1}{4} + 1\frac{3}{8}$ **b** $\frac{1}{4} + \frac{5}{8}$

a Start at $2\frac{1}{4}$ on the fraction chart. Add 1 to take you to $3\frac{1}{4}$. Then count on $\frac{3}{8}$ to $3\frac{5}{8}$.

b Start at $\frac{1}{4}$ on the number line and count on $\frac{5}{8}$ to take you to $\frac{7}{8}$.

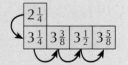

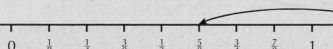

0 $\frac{1}{8}$ $\frac{1}{4}$ $\frac{3}{8}$ $\frac{1}{2}$ $\frac{5}{8}$ $\frac{3}{4}$ $\frac{7}{8}$

Example 4.7

Subtract the following fractions: **a** $2\frac{1}{4} - 1\frac{3}{8}$ **b** $1\frac{1}{4} - \frac{5}{8}$

a Start at $2\frac{1}{4}$ on the fraction chart. Subtract 1 to take you to $1\frac{1}{4}$. Then count back $\frac{3}{8}$ to $\frac{7}{8}$.

b Start at $1\frac{1}{4}$ on the number line and count back $\frac{5}{8}$ to take you to $\frac{5}{8}$.

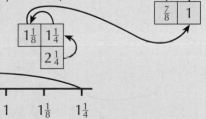

0 $\frac{1}{8}$ $\frac{1}{4}$ $\frac{3}{8}$ $\frac{1}{2}$ $\frac{5}{8}$ $\frac{3}{4}$ $\frac{7}{8}$ 1 $1\frac{1}{8}$ $1\frac{1}{4}$

Example 4.8 ▶ Work out each of the following: **a** $\frac{3}{7} + \frac{5}{7}$ **b** $\frac{2}{9} + \frac{5}{9} - \frac{1}{9}$

Unless you can use a fraction chart or a number line, fractions must have the same denominator before they can be added or subtracted. The numerator of the answer is just the sum (or difference) of the original numerators. The denominator does not change. Sometimes it is possible to cancel the answer to its lowest terms.

a $\frac{3}{7} + \frac{5}{7} = \frac{8}{7} = 1\frac{1}{7}$ **b** $\frac{2}{9} + \frac{5}{9} - \frac{1}{9} = \frac{6}{9} = \frac{2}{3}$

Example 4.9 ▶ Work out each of the following: **a** $\frac{2}{3}$ of 45p **b** $\frac{3}{7}$ of 140 cm

a First find $\frac{1}{3}$ of 45: 45 ÷ 3 = 15. So, $\frac{2}{3}$ of 45p = 2 × 15 = 30p.

b First find $\frac{1}{7}$ of 140: 140 ÷ 7 = 20. So, $\frac{3}{7}$ of 140 cm = 3 × 20 = 60 cm.

Exercise 4C

1 Add the following fractions. The fraction chart and the number line on page 46 may help.

a $\frac{5}{8} + \frac{1}{2}$ **b** $1\frac{1}{8} + \frac{3}{8}$ **c** $2\frac{2}{8} + 1\frac{5}{8}$ **d** $1\frac{1}{2} + \frac{7}{8}$

e $1\frac{5}{8} + 1\frac{3}{4}$ **f** $2\frac{7}{8} + 1\frac{1}{4}$ **g** $1\frac{3}{8} + 2\frac{3}{8}$ **h** $\frac{3}{8} + 1\frac{1}{2} + 1\frac{3}{4}$

2 Add the following fractions. Convert to mixed numbers or cancel down to lowest terms.

a $\frac{1}{3} + \frac{1}{3}$ **b** $\frac{5}{6} + \frac{5}{6}$ **c** $\frac{3}{10} + \frac{3}{10}$ **d** $\frac{1}{9} + \frac{2}{9}$

e $\frac{4}{15} + \frac{13}{15}$ **f** $\frac{7}{9} + \frac{5}{9}$ **g** $\frac{5}{12} + 1\frac{1}{12}$ **h** $\frac{3}{7} + \frac{5}{7} + \frac{2}{7}$

3 Subtract the following fractions. The fraction chart and the number line on page 46 may help.

a $\frac{5}{8} - \frac{1}{2}$ **b** $2\frac{1}{8} - \frac{5}{8}$ **c** $2\frac{3}{8} - 1\frac{5}{8}$ **d** $1\frac{1}{2} - \frac{7}{8}$

e $2\frac{3}{4} - 1\frac{3}{8}$ **f** $2\frac{7}{8} - 1\frac{1}{4}$ **g** $3\frac{3}{8} - 1\frac{3}{4}$ **h** $1\frac{1}{4} + 1\frac{1}{2} - 1\frac{7}{8}$

4 Subtract the following fractions. Convert to mixed numbers or cancel down to lowest terms.

a $\frac{5}{7} - \frac{2}{7}$ **b** $\frac{5}{6} - \frac{1}{6}$ **c** $\frac{9}{10} - \frac{3}{10}$ **d** $\frac{8}{9} - \frac{2}{9}$

e $\frac{14}{15} - \frac{2}{15}$ **f** $\frac{7}{9} - \frac{4}{9}$ **g** $\frac{11}{12} - \frac{5}{12}$ **h** $\frac{3}{10} + \frac{9}{10} - \frac{5}{10}$

5 Work out each of the following.

a Half of twenty-four **b** A third of thirty-six **c** A quarter of forty-four
d A sixth of eighteen **e** A fifth of thirty-five **f** An eighth of forty

6 Work out each of the following.

a $\frac{2}{3}$ of 36 m **b** $\frac{3}{4}$ of 44p **c** $\frac{5}{6}$ of £18 **d** $\frac{4}{5}$ of 35 kg

e $\frac{3}{8}$ of 40 cm **f** $\frac{3}{7}$ of 42 km **g** $\frac{4}{9}$ of 36 mm **h** $\frac{5}{6}$ of £24

i $\frac{3}{10}$ of £1 **j** $\frac{7}{8}$ of 84 m **k** $\frac{7}{12}$ of 48 cm **l** $\frac{9}{10}$ of 55 km

7 Work out each of these. Convert to mixed numbers or cancel down to lowest terms.

a $5 \times \frac{2}{3}$ **b** $3 \times \frac{3}{4}$ **c** $4 \times \frac{3}{8}$ **d** $6 \times \frac{2}{9}$

e $8 \times \frac{5}{6}$ **f** $4 \times \frac{7}{12}$ **g** $5 \times \frac{3}{7}$ **h** $4 \times \frac{3}{10}$

The Ancient Egyptians thought that 360 was a magical number because it had lots of factors.

They also used only fractions with 1 or 2 as the numerator, together with the commonly occurring fractions such as two-thirds, three-quarters, four-fifths and five-sixths.

Write down all the factors of 360 (or use your results from the extension work in Exercise 4A).

Write down the following fractions as equivalent fractions with a denominator of 360.

$$\frac{1}{2}, \frac{1}{3}, \frac{1}{4}, \frac{1}{5}, \frac{1}{6}, \frac{1}{8}, \frac{1}{9}, \frac{1}{10}, \frac{1}{12}$$

Use these results to work out:

a $\frac{1}{2} + \frac{1}{3}$ **b** $\frac{1}{2} + \frac{1}{6}$ **c** $\frac{1}{2} + \frac{1}{5}$ **d** $\frac{1}{3} + \frac{1}{4}$ **e** $\frac{1}{6} + \frac{1}{8}$

f $\frac{1}{3} - \frac{1}{5}$ **g** $\frac{1}{4} - \frac{1}{6}$ **h** $\frac{1}{8} - \frac{1}{10}$ **i** $\frac{1}{3} + \frac{1}{4} + \frac{1}{5}$ **j** $\frac{1}{6} + \frac{1}{12} - \frac{1}{4}$

Cancel down your answers to their simplest form.

Equivalences

Explain why BAG = 70%, HIDE = 2.2 and FED = $1\frac{1}{5}$.

Find the percentage value of CABBAGE. Find the decimal value of BADGE. Find the fraction value of CHIDE. Find the percentage, decimal and fraction value of other words you can make with these letters.

Example 4.10

Work out the equivalent fraction, decimal and/or percentage for each of the following.

a 0.14   **b** 0.55   **c** 66%   **d** 45%   **e** $\frac{9}{25}$ **f** $\frac{3}{8}$

a $0.14 = 14\% = \frac{14}{100} = \frac{7}{50}$ **b** $0.55 = 55\% = \frac{55}{100} = \frac{11}{20}$

c $66\% = 0.66 = \frac{66}{100} = \frac{33}{50}$ **d** $45\% = 0.45 = \frac{45}{100} = \frac{9}{20}$

d $\frac{9}{25} = \frac{36}{100} = 36\% = 0.36$ **f** $\frac{3}{8} = \frac{37.5}{100} = 37\frac{1}{2}\% = 0.375$

Example 4.11

Work out: **a** 35% of 620   **b** 40% of 56

a 10% of 620 = 62, 5% of 620 = 31. So 35% of 620 = 62 + 62 + 62 + 31 = 217.

b 10% of 56 = 5.6. So, 40% of 56 = 4 × 5.6 = 22.4.

1 Work out the equivalent percentage and fraction to each of these decimals.

a 0.3 b 0.44 c 0.65 d 0.8 e 0.78

f 0.27 g 0.05 h 0.16 i 0.96 j 0.25

2 Work out the equivalent decimal and fraction to each of these percentages.

a 35% b 70% c 48% d 40% e 64%

f 31% g 4% h 75% i 18% j 110%

3 Work out the equivalent percentage and decimal to teach of these fractions.

a $\frac{2}{25}$ b $\frac{7}{50}$ c $\frac{9}{10}$ d $\frac{17}{20}$ e $\frac{1}{8}$

f $\frac{3}{5}$ g $\frac{17}{25}$ h $1\frac{3}{4}$ i $\frac{1}{10}$ j $\frac{19}{20}$

4 Write down the equivalent decimal and percentage to each of these.

a $\frac{1}{3}$ b $\frac{2}{3}$

5 Calculate:

a 10% of 240 b 35% of 460 c 60% of 150 d 40% of 32

e 15% of 540 f 20% of 95 g 45% of 320 h 5% of 70

i 75% of 280 j 10% of 45 k 30% of 45

Extension Work

As a decimal, a fraction and a percentage are all different ways of writing the same thing, we can sometimes make a calculation easier by using an equivalent form instead of the decimal, fraction or percentage given.

Example 1: 20% of 35. As 20% is $\frac{1}{5}$, this is the same as $\frac{1}{5} \times 35 = 7$.

Example 2: 0.3×340. As 0.3 is 30%, this the same as 30% of 340. 10% of 340 is 34. So, 30% of 340 is $3 \times 34 = 102$.

Example 3: $\frac{3}{25}$ of 40. As $\frac{3}{25}$ is 0.12, this is the same as $0.12 \times 40 = 4.8$.

Rewrite the following using an alternative to the percentage, decimal or fraction given. Then work out the answer.

a 20% of 75 b $\frac{2}{25}$ of 60 c 25% of 19 d 60% of 550

e $\frac{3}{20}$ of 90 f 0.125×64 g $\frac{3}{5}$ of 7 h 0.4×270

i 75% of 44 j 0.3333×180

Solving problems

Mrs Bountiful decided to give £10 000 to her grandchildren, nieces and nephews. She gave $\frac{1}{5}$ to her only grandson, $\frac{1}{8}$ to each of her two granddaughters, $\frac{1}{10}$ to each of her three nieces and $\frac{1}{20}$ to each of her four nephews. What was left she gave to charity. How much did they each receive? What **fraction** of the £10 000 did she give to charity?

The best way to do this problem is to work with amounts of money rather than fractions.

The grandson gets $\frac{1}{5} \times$ £10 000 = £2000. Each granddaughter gets $\frac{1}{8} \times$ £10 000 = £1250. Each niece gets $\frac{1}{10} \times$ £10 000 = £1000. Each nephew gets $\frac{1}{20} \times$ £10 000 = £500.

Altogether she gives away $2000 + 2 \times (1250) + 3 \times (1000) + 4 \times (500) = £9500$. This leaves £500. As a fraction of £10 000, this is $\frac{500}{10\,000} = \frac{1}{20}$.

Solve the problems in Exercise 4E. Show all your working and explain what you are doing.

1 What number is halfway between the two numbers shown on each scale?

a
$\frac{1}{6}$ $\frac{5}{9}$

b
$\frac{1}{10}$ $\frac{9}{20}$

c
$1\frac{1}{4}$ $2\frac{3}{8}$

2 Which of these is greater?

a $\frac{3}{5}$ of 45 or $\frac{2}{3}$ of 39?   b $\frac{3}{4}$ of 64 or $\frac{7}{9}$ of 63?   c $\frac{3}{10}$ of 35 or $\frac{1}{4}$ of 39?

3 There are 360 passengers on a Jumbo Jet. $\frac{1}{4}$ of them are British, $\frac{2}{5}$ of them are French, $\frac{1}{6}$ of them are German, $\frac{1}{12}$ of them are Italian and the rest are Dutch. How many of each nationality are there? What fraction of the passengers are Dutch?

4 Which of these dealers is giving the better value?

Jack's Fita Duo!

$\frac{1}{6}$ off the normal price of £45 000

Jill's Fita Duo!

$\frac{1}{5}$ off the normal price of £48,000

5 $\frac{4}{15}$ and $\frac{24}{9}$ are examples of three-digit fractions.

a There is only one three-digit fraction equal to $1\frac{1}{2}$. What is it?

b There are three three-digit fractions equal to $2\frac{1}{2}$, $3\frac{1}{2}$ and $4\frac{1}{2}$. Find them and explain why there cannot be more than three equivalent three-digit fractions for these numbers.

c In the series of fractions $2\frac{1}{2}$, $3\frac{1}{2}$, $4\frac{1}{2}$, $5\frac{1}{2}$, ..., the last one that has three equivalent three-digit fractions is $16\frac{1}{2}$. Explain why.

6 There are 54 fractions in the sequence: $\frac{1}{54}$, $\frac{2}{54}$, $\frac{3}{54}$, $\frac{4}{54}$, ..., $\frac{54}{54}$. How many of them will not cancel down to a simpler form?

7 A shop is taking 10% off all its prices. How much will these items cost after a 10% reduction?

a Saucepan £16.00   b Spoon 60p   c Coffee pot £5.80

d Bread maker £54.00   e Cutlery set £27.40   f Tea set £20.80

8 A company is offering its workers a 5% pay rise. How much will the salary of each of the following people be after the pay rise?

a Fred the storeman £12 000   b Alice the office manager £25 000

c Doris the director £40 000   d John the driver £15 500

9 Another company is offering its workers a 4% or £700 per annum pay rise, whichever is the greater.

What will the pay of the following people be after the pay rise?

a Alf the storeman £12 000

b Mark the office manager £25 000

c Joe the driver £15 500

d At what salary will a 4% pay rise be the same as a £700 pay rise?

National Curriculum SATs questions

LEVEL 4

1 *1997 Paper 1*

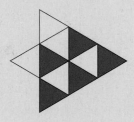
Diagram A

Diagram B

Diagram C

$\frac{1}{2}$ of diagram A is shaded.

a What fraction of shape B is shaded? What percentage of shape B is shaded?

b Copy and shade $\frac{2}{5}$ of shape C. What percentage of shape C have you shaded?

2 *2000 Paper 1*

A pupil recorded how much rain fell on 5 different days.

a Copy the statements and fill in the gaps with the correct day

The most rain fell on ....

The least rain fell on ....

	Amount in cm
Monday	0.2
Tuesday	0.8
Wednesday	0.5
Thursday	0.25
Friday	0.05

b How much more rain fell on Wednesday than on Thursday?

c How much rain fell altogether on Monday, Tuesday and Wednesday?

Now write your answer in millimetres.

3 *2001 Paper 1*

a Look at these fractions: $\frac{1}{2}$ $\frac{1}{3}$ $\frac{5}{6}$

Copy the number line and mark each fraction on it.

The first one has been done for you.

b Copy the fractions and fill in the missing numbers.

$$\frac{2}{12} = \frac{\boxed{}}{6} \qquad \frac{1}{2} = \frac{2}{\boxed{}} \qquad \frac{12}{\boxed{}} = \frac{6}{24}$$

LEVEL 5

4 *1998 Paper 1*

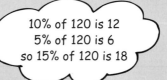

This is how Caryl works out 15% of 120 in her head.

a Show how Caryl can work out $17\frac{1}{2}$ % of 240 in her head.

b Work out 35% of 520. Show your working.

5 *2001 Paper 1*

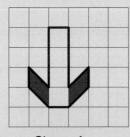
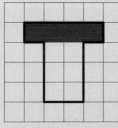
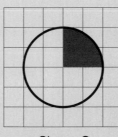
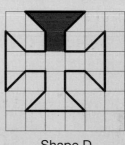

Shape A   Shape B   Shape C   Shape D

a What fraction of shape A is shaded?

b What percentage of shape B is shaded?

c Which of shape C or shape D has the greater percentage shaded or are they both the same?

Explain how you know.

CHAPTER 5

Handling Data **1**

This chapter is going to show you

- how to calculate the mode, the median, the mean and the range for a set of data
- how to interpret statistical diagrams and charts
- how to use the probability scale
- how to collect data from experiments and calculate probabilities

What you should already know

- How to interpret data from tables, graphs and charts
- How to draw line graphs, frequency tables and bar charts

Mode, median and range

Statistics is concerned with the collection and organisation of data, the representation of data on diagrams and the interpretation of data.

When interpreting data we often need to find an **average**. For example: the average rainfall in Britain, the average score of a batsman, the average weekly wage, the average mark in an examination.

An average is a useful statistic because it represents a whole set of values by just a single or typical value. This section explains how to find two types of average: the **mode** and the **median**. It also explains how to find the **range** of a set of values.

The **mode** is the value that occurs most often in a set of data. It is the only average that can be used for non-numerical data. Sometimes there may be no mode because either all the values are different, or no single value occurs more often than other values. For grouped data, a mode cannot be found, so, instead, we find the **modal class**.

The **median** is the middle value for a set of values when they are put in numerical order. It is often used when one value in the set of data is much larger or much smaller than the rest. This value is called a **rogue value**.

The **range** of a set of values is the largest value minus the smallest value. A small range means that the values in the set of data are similar in size, whereas a large range means that the values differ a lot and therefore are more spread out.

Example 5.1 ▷

Here are the ages of 11 players in a football squad. Find the mode, median and range.

23, 19, 24, 26, 27, 27, 24, 23, 20, 23, 26

First, put the ages in order: 19, 20, 23, 23, 23, 24, 24, 26, 26, 27, 27

The mode is the number which occurs most often. So, the mode is 23.

The median is the number in the middle of the set. So, the median is 24.

The range is the largest number minus the smallest number: 27 − 19 = 8. The range is 8.

Example 5.2 ▶

Below are the marks of ten pupils in a mental arithmetic test. Find the mode, median and range.

> 19, 18, 16, 15, 13, 14, 20, 19, 18, 15

First, put the marks in order: 13, 14, 15, 15, 16, 18, 18, 19, 19, 20

There is no mode because no number occurs more often than the others.

There are two numbers in the middle of the set: 16 and 18. The median is the number in the middle of these two numbers. So, the median is 17.

The range is the largest number minus the smallest number: 20 – 13 = 7. The range is 7.

Exercise 5A

1 Find the mode of each of the following sets of data.

    a   red, white, blue, red, white, blue, red, blue, white, red

    b   rain, sun, cloud, fog, rain, sun, snow, cloud, snow, sun, rain, sun

    c   E, A, I, U, E, O, I, E, A, E, A, O, I, U, E, I, E

    d   ♠, ♣, ♥, ♦, ♣, ♠, ♥, ♣, ♦, ♥, ♣, ♥, ♦, ♥

2 Find the median of each of the following sets of data.

    a   7, 6, 2, 3, 1, 9, 5, 4, 8

    b   36, 34, 45, 28, 37, 40, 24, 27, 33, 31, 41

    c   14, 12, 18, 6, 10, 20, 16, 8

    d   99, 101, 107, 103, 109, 102, 105, 110, 100, 98

3 Find the range of each of the following sets of data.

    a   23, 37, 18, 23, 28, 19, 21, 25, 36

    b   3, 1, 2, 3, 1, 0, 4, 2, 4, 2, 6, 5, 4, 5

    c   2.1, 3.4, 2.7, 1.8, 2.3, 2.6, 2.9, 1.7, 2.2

    d   2, 1, 3, 0, –2, 3, –1, 1, 0, –2, 1

4 Find the mode, median and range of each set of data.

    a   £2.50   £1.80   £3.65   £3.80   £4.20   £3.25   £1.80

    b   23 kg, 18 kg, 22 kg, 31 kg, 29 kg, 32 kg

    c   132 cm, 145 cm, 151cm, 132 cm, 140 cm, 142 cm

    d   32°, 36°, 32°, 30°, 31°, 31°, 34°, 33°, 32°, 35°

5 A group of nine Year 7 students had their lunch in the school cafeteria. Given below is the amount that each of them spent.

    £2.30   £2.20   £2.00   £2.50   £2.20
    £2.90   £3.60   £2.20   £2.80

    a   Find the mode for the data.

    b   Find the median for the data.

    c   Which is the better average to use? Explain your answer.

6 Mr Kent draws a grouped frequency table to show the marks obtained by 32 students in his science test.

Mark	Tally	Frequency
21–40	卌	
41–60	卌 IIII	
61–80	卌 卌 I	
81–100	卌 II	

a Copy and complete the frequency column in the table.

b Write down the modal class for Mr Kent's data.

c What is the greatest range of marks possible for the data in the table?

d Explain why it is not possible to find the exact median for the data in the table.

7 a Write down a list of seven numbers which has a median of 10 and a mode of 12.

b Write down a list of eight numbers which has a median of 10 and a mode of 12.

c Write down a list of seven numbers which has a median of 10, a mode of 12 and a range of 8.

Extension Work

Surveys

Carry out a survey for any of the following. For each one, collect your data on a survey sheet, find the modal category and draw diagrams to illustrate your data.

1 The most popular colour of cars in the staff car park.

2 The most common letter in a page of text.

3 The favourite TV soap opera of students in your class.

The mean

The **mean** is the most commonly used average. It is also called the **mean average** or simply the **average**. The mean can be used only with numerical data.

The mean of a set of values is the sum of all the values divided by the number of values in the set. That is:

$$\text{Mean} = \frac{\text{Sum of all values}}{\text{Number of values}}$$

The mean is a useful statistic because it takes all values into account, but it can be distorted by rogue values.

Example 5.3

Find the mean of 2, 7, 9, 10.

$$\text{Mean} = \frac{2 + 7 + 9 + 10}{4} = \frac{28}{4} = 7$$

For more complex data, we can use a calculator. When the answer is not exact, the mean is usually given to one decimal place (1 dp).

Example 5.4 ▶

The ages of seven people are 40, 37, 34, 42, 45, 39, 35. Calculate their mean age.

$$\text{Mean age} = \frac{40 + 37 + 34 + 42 + 45 + 39 + 35}{7} = \frac{272}{7} = 38.9 \text{ (1dp)}$$

The mean can also be calculated from a frequency table, as the following example shows.

Example 5.5 ▶

The frequency table shows the scores obtained when a dice is thrown 20 times. Find the mean score.

Score	1	2	3	4	5	6
Frequency	4	3	4	3	2	4

The table is redrawn in the way shown on the right in order to calculate the sum of the 20 scores.

Score	Frequency	Score × Frequency
1	4	4
2	3	6
3	4	12
4	3	12
5	2	10
6	4	24
Total	**20**	**68**

$$\text{Mean score} = \frac{68}{20} = 3.4$$

Exercise 5B

1 Find the mean of each of the following sets of data.

   a 8, 7, 6, 10, 4   **b** 23, 32, 40, 37, 29, 25

   c 11, 12, 9, 26, 14, 17, 16   **d** 2.4, 1.6, 3.2, 1.8, 4.2, 2.5, 4.5, 2.2

2 Find the mean of each of the following sets of data, giving your answer to 1 dp.

   a 6, 7, 6, 4, 2, 3   **b** 12, 15, 17, 11, 18, 16, 14

   c 78, 72, 82, 95, 47, 67, 77, 80   **d** 9.1, 7.8, 10.3, 8.5, 11.6, 8.9

3 The heights, in centimetres, of ten children are

      132, 147, 143, 136, 135, 146, 153, 132, 137, 149

   a Find the mean height of the children.

   b Find the median height of the children.

   c Find the modal height of the children.

   d Which average do you think is the best one to use? Explain your answer.

4 The weekly wages of 12 office staff in a small company are

£120, £140, £110, £400, £105, £360, £150, £200, £120, £130, £125, £140

a Find the mean weekly wage of the staff.

b How many staff earn more than the mean wage?

c Explain why so few staff earn more than the mean wage.

5 The frequency table shows the shoe sizes of 30 students in form 7HW.

Shoe size	3	4	5	6	7	8
Frequency	3	3	8	9	6	1

Calculate the mean shoe size of the form.

6 The bar chart shows the midday temperatures for every day in February for Playa de las Américas in Tenerife.

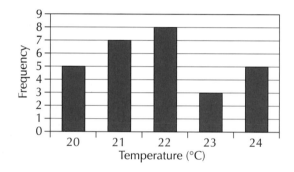

By drawing a suitable frequency table, calculate the mean daily temperature.

7 a
6	4	3	7

Find the mean of the four cards.

b
3	7	6	8	?

Find the value of the fifth card, if the mean of the five cards is to be the same as in part **a**.

8 The mean age of three friends, Phil, Martin and Mike, is 42. Steve joins the three and the mean age of the four friends is now 40. How old is Steve?

Extension Work

1 Vital statistics

Working in groups, calculate the mean for the group's age, height and weight.

2 Average score

Throw a dice ten times. Record your results on a survey sheet. What is the mean score?

Repeat the experiment but throw the dice 20 times. What is the mean score now?

Repeat the experiment but throw the dice 50 times. What is the mean score now?

Write down anything you notice as you throw the dice more times.

Statistical diagrams

Once data has been collected from a survey, it can de displayed in various ways to make it easier to understand and interpret.

The most common ways to display data are bar charts, pie charts and line graphs.

Bar charts have several different forms. The questions in Exercise 5C will show you the different types of bar chart that can be used. Notice that data which has single categories gives a bar chart with gaps between the bars. Grouped data gives a bar chart with no gaps between the bars.

Pie charts are used to show data when you do not need to know the number of items in each category of the sample. Pie charts are used to show proportions.

Line graphs are usually used to show trends and patterns in the data.

Exercise 5C

1 The bar chart shows how the students in class 7PB travel to school.

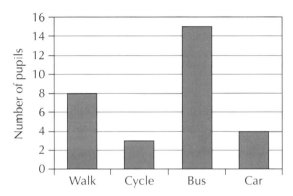

a How many students cycle to school?

b What is the mode for the way the students travel to school?

c How many students are there in class 7PB?

2 The dual bar chart shows the daily average number of hours of sunshine in London and Edinburgh over a year.

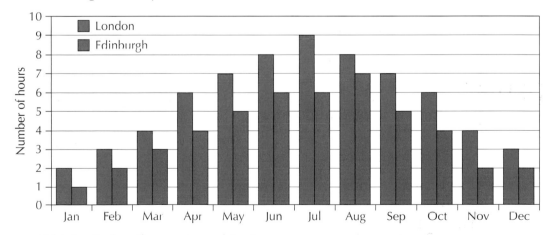

a Which city has the most sunshine?

b Which month is the sunniest for **i** London **ii** Edinburgh?

c What is the range for the number of hours of sunshine over the year for
i London **ii** Edinburgh?

d Assume the total number of male teachers will be about the same as the total number of female teachers.

Use the chart to decide which statement is correct.

Generally, male teachers will tend to be younger than female teachers.

Generally, female teachers will tend to be younger than male teachers.

Explain how you used the chart to decide.

3 *2000 Paper 2*

In each box of cereal there is a free gift of a card.

You cannot tell which card will be in a box. Each card is equally likely.

There are four different cards: A, B, C or D

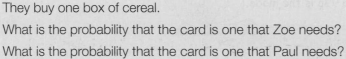

a Zoe needs card A.

Her brother Paul needs cards C and D.

They buy one box of cereal.

What is the probability that the card is one that Zoe needs?

What is the probability that the card is one that Paul needs?

b Then their mother opens the box. She tells them the card is not card A.

Now what is the probability the card is one that Zoe needs?

What is the probability that the card is one that Paul needs?

This chapter is going to show you

- how to use letters in place of numbers
- how to use the rules (conventions) of algebra
- how to solve puzzles called equations
- how to solve problems using algebra.

What you should already know

- Understand and be able to apply the rules of arithmetic
- The meaning of the words term and expression

Algebraic terms and expressions

In algebra, you will keep meeting three words: **variable**, **term** and **expression**.

Variable This is the letter in a term or an expression whose value can vary. Some of the letters most used for variables are x, y, n and t.

Term This is an algebraic quantity which contains only a letter (or combination of letters) and may contain a number. For example:

$3n$ means 3 multiplied by the variable n

$\dfrac{n}{2}$ means n divided by 2

n^2 means n multiplied by itself (normally said as 'n squared')

Expression This is a combination of letters (variables) and signs, often with numbers. For example:

$8 - n$ means subtract n from 8

$n - 3$ means subtract 3 from n

$2n + 7$ means n multiplied by 2 with 7 added on

When you give a particular value to the variable in an expression, the expression takes on a particular value.

For example, if the variable n takes the value of 4, then the terms and expressions which include this variable will have particular values, as shown below:

$$3n = 12 \quad \frac{n}{2} = 2 \quad n^2 = 16 \quad 8 - n = 4 \quad n - 3 = 1 \quad 2n + 7 = 15$$

Exercise 6A

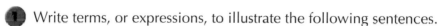

1 Write terms, or expressions, to illustrate the following sentences.

a Add four to m.　　b Multiply t by eight.　　c Nine minus y.

d Multiply m by itself.　　e Divide n by five.　　f Subtract t from seven.

g Multiply n by three, then add five.　　h Multiply six by t.

i Multiply m by five, then subtract three.　　j Multiply x by x.

2 Write down the values of each term for the three values of n.

a $4n$ where   i $n = 2$ ii $n = 5$ iii $n = 11$

b $\dfrac{n}{2}$ where   i $n = 6$ ii $n = 14$ iii $n = 8$

c n^2 where   i $n = 3$ ii $n = 6$ iii $n = 7$

d $3n$ where   i $n = 7$ ii $n = 5$ iii $n = 9$

e $\dfrac{n}{5}$ where   i $n = 10$ ii $n = 5$ iii $n = 20$

f $9n$ where   i $n = 2$ ii $n = 4$ iii $n = 8$

g $\dfrac{n}{10}$ where   i $n = 20$ ii $n = 50$ iii $n = 100$

3 Write down the values of each expression for the three values of n.

a $n + 7$ where   i $n = 3$ ii $n = 4$ iii $n = 12$

b $n - 5$ where   i $n = 8$ ii $n = 14$ iii $n = 11$

c $10 - n$ where   i $n = 4$ ii $n = 7$ iii $n = 1$

d $2n + 3$ where   i $n = 2$ ii $n = 5$ iii $n = 7$

e $5n - 1$ where   i $n = 3$ ii $n = 4$ iii $n = 8$

f $20 - 2n$ where   i $n = 1$ ii $n = 5$ iii $n = 9$

g $4n + 5$ where   i $n = 4$ ii $n = 3$ iii $n = 7$

4 Write down the values of each expression for the three values of n.

a $n^2 - 1$ where   i $n = 2$ ii $n = 3$ iii $n = 4$

b $n^2 + 1$ where   i $n = 5$ ii $n = 6$ iii $n = 7$

c $5 + n^2$ where   i $n = 8$ ii $n = 9$ iii $n = 10$

d $n^2 + 9$ where   i $n = 5$ ii $n = 4$ iii $n = 3$

e $25 + n^2$ where   i $n = 4$ ii $n = 5$ iii $n = 6$

Extension Work

1 Using the variable n and the operations add, subtract, multiply, divide, square, write down as many different expressions as you can that use:

a two operations

b three operations

2 Choose any value for n, say 5, and see how many of these expressions have the same value.

Rules of algebra

The rules (conventions) of algebra are the same rules that are used in arithmetic.
For example:

$3 + 4 = 4 + 3$ $a + b = b + a$
$3 \times 4 = 4 \times 3$ $a \times b = b \times a$ or $ab = ba$

But remember, for example, that:

$7 - 5 \neq 5 - 7$ $a - b \neq b - a$
$6 \div 3 \neq 3 \div 6$ $\dfrac{a}{b} \neq \dfrac{b}{a}$

From one fact, other facts can be stated. For example:

$3 + 4 = 7$

gives $7 - 4 = 3$ and $7 - 3 = 4$

$3 \times 4 = 12$

gives $\dfrac{12}{3} = 4$ and $\dfrac{12}{4} = 3$

$a + b = 10$

gives $10 - a = b$ and $10 - b = a$

$ab = 10$

gives $\dfrac{10}{a} = b$ and $\dfrac{10}{b} = a$

Exercise 6B

1 In each of the following clouds only two expressions are equal to each other. Write down the equal pair.

a

$3 + 5 \qquad 3 - 5$

$3 \times 5 \qquad 5 + 3$

$5 \div 3 \qquad 5 - 3$

b

$2 + 7 \qquad 7 - 2$

$2 \times 7 \qquad 7 \div 2 \qquad 2 \div 7$

7×2

c

$a + b \qquad a - b$

$a \times b \qquad b + a$

$b \div a \qquad b - a$

d

$m + p \qquad m - p$

$m \times p \qquad p \div m \qquad m \div p$

$p \times m$

2 In each of the following lists, write down all the expressions that equal each other.

a $5 + 6, \ 5 \times 6, \ 6 - 5, \ 6 \times 5, \ 6 \div 5, \ 5 - 6, \ 6 + 5, \ 5 \div 6$

b $ab, \ a + b, \ b - a, \ ba, \ a/b, \ a - b, \ b/a, \ b + a, \ a \div b$

c $k \times t, \ k + t, \ k/t, \ kt, \ k \div t, \ tk, \ t + k, \ t \times k, \ k - t$

3 Write down two more facts that are implied by each of the following statements.

a $2 + 8 = 10$ **b** $a + b = 7$ **c** $3 \times 5 = 15$ **d** $ab = 24$

e $3 + k = 9$ **f** $m + 4 = 5$ **g** $2n = 6$ **h** $\dfrac{8}{a} = 7$

4 Show by the substitution of suitable numbers that:

a $m + n = n + m$ **b** $ab = ba$ **c** $p - t \neq t - p$ **d** $\dfrac{m}{n} \neq \dfrac{n}{m}$

5 Show by the substitution of suitable numbers that:

a If $a + b = 7$, then $7 - a = b$ **b** If $ab = 12$, then $a = \dfrac{12}{b}$

6 Show by the substitution of suitable numbers that:

a $a + b + c = c + b + a$ **b** $acb = abc = cba$

7 If you know that $a + b + c + d = 180$, write down as many other expressions that equal 180 as you can.

8 It is known that $abcd = 100$. Write down at least ten other expressions that must also equal 100.

1   Write down some values of a and b which make the following statement true.

   $a + b = ab$

   You will find only one pair of integers. There are lots of decimal numbers
   to find, but each time try to keep one of the variables an integer.

2   Write down some values of a and b which make the following statements true.

   $a - b = \dfrac{a}{b}$

   You will find only one pair of integers. There are lots of decimal numbers
   to find, but each time try to keep one of the variables an integer.

3   Does $(a + b) \times (a - b) = a^2 - b^2$ work for all values of a and b?

Simplifying expressions

If you add 2 cups to 3 cups, you get 5 cups.
In algebra, this can be represented as

   $2c + 3c = 5c$

The terms here are called **like terms**, because they are all multiples of c.

Only like terms can be added or subtracted to simply an expression. Unlike terms cannot
be combined.

Check out these two boxes.

Examples of combining like terms
$3p + 4p = 7p$ $5t + 3t = 8t$
$9w - 4w = 5w$ $12q - 5q = 7q$
$a + 3a + 7a = 11a$
$15m - 2m - m = 12m$

Examples of unlike terms
$x + y$ $2m + 3p$
$7 - 3y$ $5g + 2k$
$m - 3p$

Like terms can be combined even when they are mixed together with unlike terms.
For example:

   2 apples and 1 pear added to 4 apples and 2 kiwis make 6 apples, 1 pear and
   2 kiwis, or in algebra

   $2a + p + 4a + 2k = 6a + 2k + p$

Examples of different sorts of like terms mixed together
$4t + 5m + 2m + 3t + m = 7t + 8m$
$5k + 4g - 2k - g = 3k + 3g$

NOTE $g = 1g$ $m = 1m$

You **never** write the one in
front of a variable

There are many situations in algebra where there is a need to use brackets in expressions. They keep things tidy! You can **expand** brackets, as shown in Examples 6.1 and 6.2. This operation is also called **multiplying out**.

Example 6.1 ▷

Expand $3(a + 5)$.

This means that each term in the brackets is multiplied by the number outside the brackets. This gives

$$3 \times a + 3 \times 5 = 3a + 15$$

Example 6.2 ▷

Expand and simplify $2(3p + 4) + 3(4p + 1)$.

This means that each term in each pair of brackets is multiplied by the number outside the brackets. This gives

$$2 \times 3p + 2 \times 4 + 3 \times 4p + 3 \times 1$$
$$= 6p + 8 + 12p + 3$$
$$= 18p + 11$$

Exercise 6C

1 Simplify each of the following expressions.

a $4c + 2c$ b $6d + 4d$ c $7p - 5p$ d $2x + 6x + 3x$

e $4t + 2t - t$ f $7m - 3m$ g $q + 5q - 2q$ h $a + 6a - 3a$

i $4p + p - 2p$ j $2w + 3w - w$ k $4t + 3t - 5t$ l $5g - g - 2g$

2 Simplify each of the following expressions.

a $2x + 2y + 3x + 6y$ b $4w + 6t - 2w - 2t$ c $4m + 7n + 3m - n$

d $4x + 8y - 2y - 3x$ e $8 + 4x - 3 + 2x$ f $8p + 9 - 3p - 4$

g $2y + 4x - 3 + x - y$ h $5d + 8c - 4c + 7$ i $4f + 2 + 3d - 1 - 3f$

j $8c + 7 - 7c - 4$ k $2p + q + 3p - q$ l $3t + 9 - t$

3 Expand each of the following expressions.

a $4(x + 5)$ b $2(3t + 4)$ c $5(3m + 1)$ d $4(3w - 2)$

e $6(3m - 4)$ f $7(4q - 3)$ g $2(3x - 4)$ h $3(2t + 7)$

i $7(3k + p - 2)$ j $4(3 - k + 2t)$ k $5(m - 3 + 6p)$ l $4(2 - 5k - 2m)$

4 Expand and simplify each of the following expressions.

a $4(x + 5) + 3(x + 3)$ b $5(p + 7) + 3(p + 3)$

c $3(w + 3) + 4(w - 2)$ d $6(d + 3) + 3(d - 5)$

e $3(8p + 2) + 3(5p + 1)$ f $4(6m + 5) + 2(5m - 4)$

g $5(3w + 7) + 2(2w - 1)$ h $7(3c + 2) + 2(5c - 4)$

i $4(t + 6) + 3(4t - 1)$ j $5(3x + 2) + 4(3x - 2)$

You will usually solve these types of equation by subtracting or adding to both sides in order to have a single term on each side of the equals sign.

Example 6.5 ▷

Solve $4x + 3 = 31$.

Subtract 3 from both sides: $4x + 3 - 3 = 31 - 3$

$$4x = 28$$
$$(4 \times ? = 28)$$
$$x = 7$$

Example 6.6 ▷

Solve $3x - 5 = 13$.

Add 5 to both sides: $3x - 5 + 5 = 13 + 5$

$$3x = 18$$
$$(3 \times ? = 18)$$
$$x = 6$$

Exercise 6E

1 Solve each of the following equations.

a $2x = 10$	**b** $3x = 18$	**c** $5x = 15$	**d** $4x = 8$
e $3m = 12$	**f** $5m = 30$	**g** $7m = 14$	**h** $4m = 20$
i $6k = 12$	**j** $5k = 25$	**k** $3k = 27$	**l** $2k = 16$
m $7x = 21$	**n** $4x = 28$	**p** $5x = 40$	**q** $9x = 54$

2 Solve each of the following equations.

a $x + 2 = 7$	**b** $x + 3 = 9$	**c** $x + 8 = 10$	**d** $x + 1 = 5$
e $m + 3 = 7$	**f** $m - 3 = 5$	**g** $k - 2 = 9$	**h** $p - 5 = 9$
i $k + 7 = 15$	**j** $k - 1 = 3$	**k** $m + 3 = 9$	**l** $x - 3 = 7$
m $x + 8 = 9$	**n** $n - 2 = 6$	**p** $m - 5 = 8$	**q** $x + 12 = 23$

3 Solve each of the following equations.

a $2x + 3 = 11$	**b** $2x + 5 = 13$	**c** $3x + 4 = 19$	**d** $3x + 7 = 19$
e $4m + 1 = 21$	**f** $5k + 6 = 21$	**g** $4n + 9 = 17$	**h** $2x + 7 = 27$
i $6h + 5 = 23$	**j** $3t + 5 = 26$	**k** $8x + 3 = 35$	**l** $5y + 3 = 28$
m $7x + 3 = 10$	**n** $4t + 7 = 39$	**p** $3x + 8 = 20$	**q** $8m + 5 = 21$

4 Solve each of the following equations.

a $3x - 2 = 13$	**b** $2m - 5 = 1$	**c** $4x - 1 = 11$	**d** $5t - 3 = 17$
e $2x - 3 = 13$	**f** $4m - 5 = 19$	**g** $3m - 2 = 10$	**h** $7x - 3 = 25$
i $5m - 2 = 18$	**j** $3k - 4 = 5$	**k** $8x - 5 = 11$	**l** $2t - 3 = 7$
m $4x - 3 = 5$	**n** $8y - 3 = 29$	**p** $5x - 4 = 11$	**q** $3m - 1 = 17$

5 Solve each of the following equations.

a $2x + 3 = 11$	**b** $3x + 4 = 10$	**c** $5x - 1 = 29$	**d** $4x - 3 = 25$
e $3m - 2 = 13$	**f** $5m + 4 = 49$	**g** $7m + 3 = 24$	**h** $4m - 5 = 23$
i $6k + 1 = 25$	**j** $5k - 3 = 2$	**k** $3k - 1 = 23$	**l** $2k + 5 = 15$
m $7x - 3 = 18$	**n** $4x + 3 = 43$	**p** $5x + 6 = 31$	**q** $9x - 4 = 68$

What you need to know for level 4

- How to use simple formulae expressed in words
- How to solve simple equations
- Understand the rules (conventions) of algebra

What you need to know for level 5

- How to construct, express in symbolic form and use simple formulae, involving one or two operations
- How to simplify expressions and expand brackets
- How to solve equations

National Curriculum SATs questions

LEVEL 5

1 *2000 Paper 1*

The area of the shaded square is 4.
The area of the semicircle is t

The grid below shows a shape.
The area of this shape in terms of t is $4 + 2t$

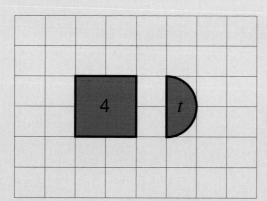

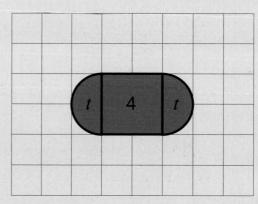

a   Write down the area of the shapes below in terms of t.

i

ii

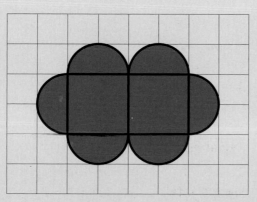

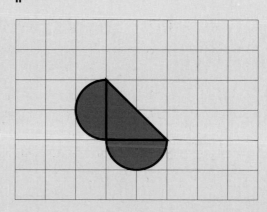

b   Draw diagrams to show shapes with area   **i** $8 + 4t$ **ii** $4 - 2t$

Jenny and Alan each have a rectangle made out of paper.

One side is 10 cm. The other side is *n* cm.

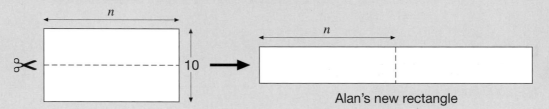

a They write expressions for the perimeter of the rectangle.

   Jenny writes 2*n* + 20

   Alan writes 2(*n* + 10)

Which of the following is a true statement?

   Jenny is correct and Alan is wrong.   Jenny is wrong and Alan is correct.

   Both Jenny and Alan are correct.   Both Jenny and Alan are wrong.

b Alan cuts his rectangle, then puts the two halves side by side.

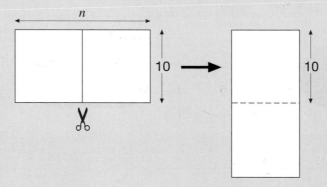

Alan's new rectangle

What is the perimeter of Alan's new rectangle? Write your expression as simply as possible.

c Jenny cuts her rectangle a different way, and puts one half below the other half.

Jenny's new rectangle

What is the perimeter of Jenny's new rectangle?

Write your expression as simply as possible.

d What value of *n* would make the perimeter of Jenny's new rectangle the same value as the perimeter of Alan's new rectangle.

This chapter is going to show you	What you should already know
○ the vocabulary and notation for lines and angles ○ how to use angles at a point, angles on a straight line, angles in a triangle and vertically opposite angles ○ how to use coordinates in all four quadrants	○ The geometric properties of triangles and quadrilaterals ○ How to plot coordinates in the first quadrant

Lines and angles

Lines   A straight line can be considered to have infinite length.

A **line segment** has finite length.

A ———————————————————————— B

The line segment AB has two end points, one at A and the other at B.

Two lines lie in a **plane**, which is a flat surface.

Two lines either are parallel or intersect.

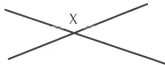

Parallel lines never meet.   These two lines intersect at a point X.   These two lines intersect at right angles. The lines are said to be **perpendicular**.

Angles   When two lines meet at a point, they form an **angle**. An angle is a measure of rotation and is measured in degrees (°).

Types of angle

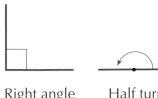

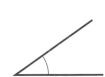

Right angle
90°

Half turn
180°

Full turn
360°

Acute angle
less than 90°

Obtuse angle
between 90° and 180°

Reflex angle
between 180° and 360°

Vertically opposite angles

When two lines intersect, the opposite angles are equal.

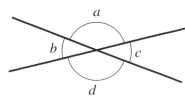

$a = d$ and $b = c$

Example 7.5 ▷

Calculate the sizes of angles d and e.

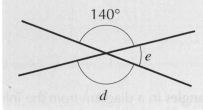

$d = 140°$ (opposite angles)
$e = 40°$ (angles on a straight line)

Exercise 7B

1 Calculate the size of each unknown angle.

a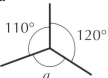

b

c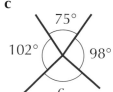

d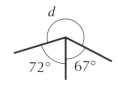

2 Calculate the size of each unknown angle.

a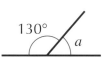

b

c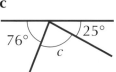

d

3 Calculate the size of each unknown angle.

a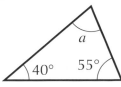

b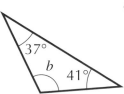

c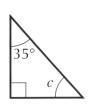

d

4 Calculate the size of each unknown angle.

a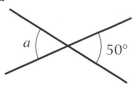

b

c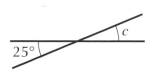

d

5 Calculate the size of each unknown angle.

a

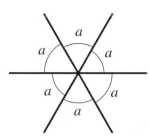

b

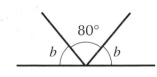

c

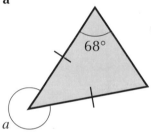

d

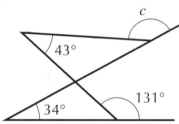

1 Calculate the size of each unknown angle.

a **b** **c**

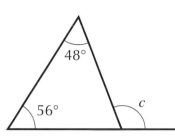

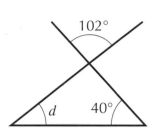

d

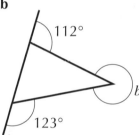

2 One angle in an isosceles triangle is 42°. Calculate the possible sizes of the other two angles.

3 Calculate the sizes of the angles marked with letters.

a **b** **c**

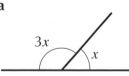

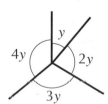

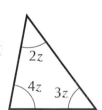

Coordinates

We use **coordinates** to locate a point on a grid.

The grid consists of two axes, called the **x-axis** and the **y-axis**. They are perpendicular to each other.

The two axes meet at a point called the **origin**, which is labelled O.

The point A on the grid is 4 units across and 3 units up.

We say that the coordinates of A are (4, 3), which is usually written as A(4, 3).

The first number, 4, is the *x*-coordinate of A and the second number, 3, is the *y*-coordinate of A. The *x*-coordinate is *always* written first.

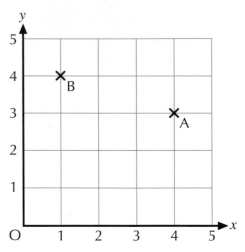

When plotting a point on a grid, a ✗ or a ● is usually used.

The coordinates of the origin are (0, 0) and the coordinates of the point B are (1, 4).

The grid system can be extended to negative numbers and points can be plotted in all **four quadrants**.

Example 7.6 ▶ The coordinates of the points on the grid are:

A(4, 2), B(–2, 3), C(–3, –1), D(1, –4)

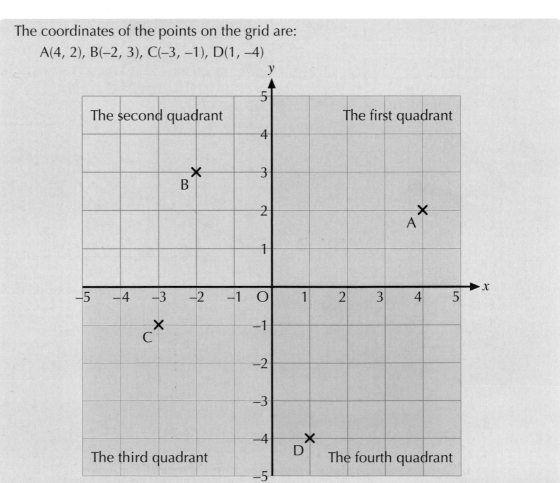

1 Write down the coordinates of the points P, Q, R, S and T.

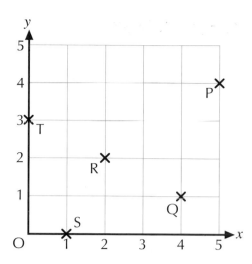

2 a Make a copy of the grid in Question 1. Then plot the points A(1, 1), B(1, 5) and C(4, 5).

b The three points are the vertices of a rectangle. Plot point D to complete the rectangle.

c Write down the coordinates of D.

3 Write down the coordinates of the points A, B, C, D, E, F, G and H.

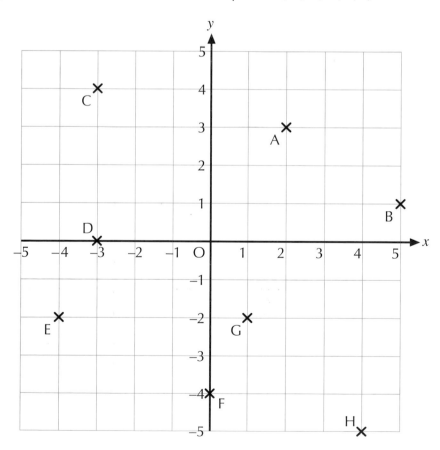

4 a Make a copy of the grid in Question 3. Then plot the points A(–4, 3), B(–2, –2), C(0, 1), D(2, –2) and E(4, 3).

b Join the points in the order given. What letter have you drawn?

1 A class did a survey on how many pencils each student had with them in school. The results of this survey are:

4, 7, 2, 18, 1, 16, 19, 15, 13, 0, 9, 17, 4, 6, 10, 12, 15, 8, 3, 14, 20, 14, 15, 18, 5, 16, 3, 6, 5, 18, 12

a Put this data into a grouped frequency table with a class size of 5: that is, 0–5, 6–10, …

b Draw a bar chart of the data.

2 A teacher asked her class: 'How many hours a week do you spend on a computer?'

She asked them to give an average, rounded figure in hours. This was their response:

3, 6, 9, 2, 23, 18, 6, 8, 29, 27, 2, 1, 0, 5, 19, 23, 30, 21, 7, 4, 23, 8, 7, 1, 0, 25, 24, 8, 13, 18, 15, 16

These are some of the reasons students gave for the length of time they spent on a computer:

'I haven't got one.' 'I play games on mine.' 'I always try to do my homework on the computer.' 'I can't use it when I want to, because my brother's always on it.'

a Put the above data into a grouped frequency table with a class size of 5.

b Draw a bar chart with the information. Try to include in the chart the reasons given.

3 Use the data you have from your survey on the number of letters in words to create a grouped frequency table:

a with a class size of 3

b with a class size of 5

c Which class size seems most sensible to use in this case?

Extension Work

Design a tally chart, with equal class sizes, to capture data in an experiment to find out how many words there are in sentences in a book.

a Use the tally chart to survey the length of sentences in a book suitable for
   i a 5-year-old   **ii** an 11-year-old   **iii** an adult

b Draw a bar chart from each frequency table.

c Comment on your results.

Data collection

Let's have a disco.

What shall we charge?
What time shall we start?
What time shall we finish?
What food shall we eat?

Let's ask a sample of the students in our school these questions. In other words, not everyone, but a few from each group.

You ask each question, then immediately complete your data collection form.

An example of a suitable data collection form is shown below.

Year group	Boy or girl	How much to charge?	Time to start?	Time to finish?	What would you like to eat?
Y7	B	£1	7 pm	11 pm	Crisps, beefburgers, chips
Y7	G	50p	7 pm	9 pm	Chips, crisps, lollies
Y8	G	£2	7.30 pm	10 pm	Crisps, hot dogs
Y11	B	£3	8.30 pm	11.30 pm	Chocolate, pizza

Keep track of the age	Try to ask equal numbers	Once the data is collected, it can be sorted into frequency tables.

There are five stages in running this type of survey:
- Deciding what questions to ask and who to ask.
- Creating a simple, suitable data collection form for all the questions.
- Asking the questions and completing the data collection form.
- After collecting all the data, collating it in frequency tables.
- Analysing the data to draw conclusions from the survey.

The size of your sample will depend on many things. It may be simply the first 50 people you come across. Or you may want 10% of the available people.

In the above example, a good sample would probably be about four from each class, two boys and two girls.

Exercise 8D

A class did the above survey on a sample of 10 students from each of the Key Stage 3 years. Their data collection chart is shown on the next page.

1 a Create the frequency tables for the suggested charges from each year group Y7, Y8 and Y9.

b Comment on the differences between the year groups.

2 a Create the frequency tables for the suggested starting times from each year group Y7, Y8 and Y9.

b Comment on the differences between the year groups.

3 a Create the frequency tables for the suggested lengths of time the disco should last from each year group Y7, Y8 and Y9.

b Comment on the differences between the year groups.

4 Complete the survey on what food each year group suggests.

Year group	Boy or girl	How much to charge	Time to start	Time to finish	What would you like to eat?
Y7	B	£1	7 pm	11 pm	Crisps, beefburgers, chips
Y7	G	50p	7 pm	9 pm	Chips, crisps, lollies
Y8	G	£2	7.30 pm	10 pm	Crisps, hot dogs
Y9	B	£3	8.30 pm	11.30 pm	Chocolate, pizza
Y9	G	£2	8 pm	10 pm	Pizza
Y9	B	£2.50	7.30 pm	9.30 pm	Hot dogs, Chocolate
Y8	G	£1	8 pm	10.30 pm	Crisps
Y7	B	75p	7 pm	9 pm	Crisps, beefburgers
Y7	B	£1	7.30 pm	10.30 pm	Crisps, lollies
Y8	B	£1.50	7 pm	9 pm	Crisps, chips, hot dogs
Y9	G	£2	8 pm	11 pm	Pizza, chocolate
Y9	G	£1.50	8 pm	10.30 pm	Chips, pizza
Y9	G	£2	8 pm	11 pm	Crisps, pizza
Y7	G	£1.50	7 pm	9 pm	Crisps, lollies, chocolate
Y8	B	£2	7.30 pm	9.30 pm	Crisps, lollies, chocolate
Y8	B	£1	8 pm	10 pm	Chips, hot dogs
Y9	B	£1.50	8 pm	11 pm	Pizza
Y7	B	50p	7 pm	9.30 pm	Crisps, hot dogs
Y8	G	75p	8 pm	10.30 pm	Crisps, chips
Y9	B	£2	7.30 pm	10.30 pm	Pizza
Y8	G	£1.50	7.30 pm	10 pm	Chips, hot dogs, chocolate
Y8	B	£1.25	7 pm	9.30 pm	Chips, hot dogs, lollies
Y9	G	£3	7 pm	9.30 pm	Crisps, pizza
Y9	B	£2.50	8 pm	10.30 pm	Crisps, hot dogs
Y7	G	25p	7.30 pm	10 pm	Crisps, beefburgers, lollies
Y7	G	50p	7 pm	9 pm	Crisps, pizza
Y7	G	£1	7 pm	9.30 pm	Crisps, pizza
Y8	B	£2	8 pm	10 pm	Crisps, chips, chocolate
Y8	G	£1.50	7.30 pm	9.30 pm	Chips, beefburgers
Y7	B	£1	7.30 pm	10 pm	Crisps, lollies

What you need to know for level 4

- How to collect discrete data and record them using frequency tables
- How to group data, where appropriate, into equal class intervals
- How to represent collected data in frequency diagrams, and interpret them

What you need to know for level 5

- How to compare two simple distributions
- How to interpret graphs and diagrams, and draw conclusions
- Recognise the need for care when setting class boundaries

National Curriculum SATs questions

LEVEL 5

1 *1997 paper 2*

Some pupils wanted to find out if people liked a new biscuit.

They decided to do a survey and wrote a questionnaire.

a One question was:

How old are you (in years)?

☐   ☐   ☐   ☐   ☐

20 or younger   20 to 30   30 to 40   40 to 50   50 or over

Mary said:

> The labels for the middle three boxes need changing.

Explain why Mary was right.

b A different question was:

How much do you usually spend on biscuits each week?

☐ A lot   ☐ A little   ☐ Nothing   ☐ Don't know

Mary said: 'Some of these labels need changing too.'
Write new labels for any boxes that need changing.
You may change as many labels as you want to.

The pupils decide to give their questionnaire to 50 people.

Jon said:

> Let's ask 50 pupils in our school.

c Give one disadvantage of Jon's suggestion.

d Give one advantage of Jon's suggestion.

CHAPTER **9** Number and Measures **3**

This chapter is going to show you

- how to round off positive whole numbers and decimals
- the order of operations
- how to multiply and divide a three-digit whole number by a two-digit whole number without a calculator
- how to use a calculator efficiently

What you should already know

- Tables up to 10 times 10
- Place value of the digits in a number such as 23.508

Rounding

What is wrong with this picture?

It shows that the woman's weight (60 kg) balances the man's weight (110 kg) when both weights are rounded to the nearest 100 kg!

This example highlights the need to round numbers *sensibly*, depending on the situation in which they occur.

But, we do not always need numbers to be precise, and it is easier to work with numbers that are rounded off.

Example 9.1 ▶ Round off each of these numbers to **i** the nearest 10 **ii** the nearest 100 **iii** the nearest 1000.

    a   937   **b**   2363   **c**   3799   **d**   281

    a   937 is 940 to nearest 10, 900 to the nearest 100 and 1000 to the nearest 1000.

    b   2363 is 2360 to nearest 10, 2400 to the nearest 100, and 2000 to the nearest 1000.

    c   3799 is 3800 to nearest 10, 3800 to the nearest 100, and 4000 to the nearest 1000.

    d   281 is 280 to nearest 10, 300 to the nearest 100, and 0 to the nearest 1000.

Example 9.2 ▷

Round off each of these numbers to **i** the nearest whole number **ii** one decimal place.

a   9.35   **b**   4.323   **c**   5.99

a   9.35 is 9 to the nearest whole number and 9.4 to 1 dp.

b   4.323 is 4 to the nearest whole number and 4.3 to 1 dp.

c   5.99 is 6 to the nearest whole number and 6.0 to 1 dp.

Exercise 9A

1 Round off each of these numbers to **i** the nearest 10 **ii** the nearest 100 **iii** the nearest 1000.

    a 3731 **b** 807   **c** 2111 **d** 4086 **e** 265   **f** 3457
    g 4050 **h** 2999 **i** 1039 **j** 192   **k** 3192 **l** 964

2 Round off each of these numbers to **i** the nearest whole number **ii** one decimal place.

    a 4.72 **b** 3.07 **c** 2.634 **d** 1.932 **e** 0.78 **f** 0.92
    g 3.92 **h** 2.64 **l** 3.18   **j** 3.475 **k** 1.45 **l** 1.863

3 **i**   What is the mass being weighed by each scale to the nearest 100 g?

    ii Estimate the mass being weighed to the nearest 10 g.

a    **b**   **c**    **d**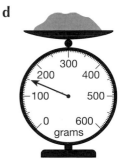

4 **i**   What is the volume of the liquid in each measuring cylinder to the nearest 10 ml?

    ii Estimate the volume of liquid to the nearest whole number.

a 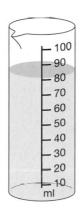   **b** 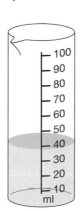   **c** 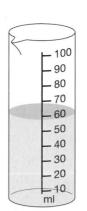   **d**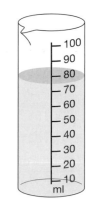

5 How long are each of these ropes to **i** the nearest 100 cm **ii** the nearest 10 cm **iii** the nearest cm **iv** the nearest mm?

a
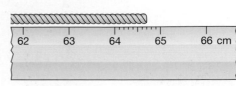

176   177   178   179 cm

b

62   63   64   65   66 cm

c

278   279   280   281   282 cm

d

3.4   3.5   3.6   3.7   3.8 m

6 **a** The following are the diameters of the planets in kilometres. Round off each one to the nearest 1000 km. Then place the planets in order of size, starting with the smallest.

Planet	Earth	Jupiter	Mars	Mercury	Neptune	Pluto	Saturn	Uranus	Venus
Diameter (km)	12 800	142 800	6780	5120	49 500	2284	120 660	51 100	12 100

b What would happen if you rounded off the diameters to the nearest 10 000 km?

Extension Work

The headteacher says: 'All of our classes have about 30 pupils in them.' Given this number is to the nearest 10, what is the smallest class there could be and what would be the largest?

The deputy head says: 'All of the cars driving past the school are doing about 30 mph.' Given this number is to the nearest 10, what is the lowest speed the cars could be doing and what would be the highest?

Why are these answers different?

Write down the smallest and largest values for each of the following.

a A crowd of people estimated at 80 to the nearest 10 people.

b The speed of a car estimated at 80 mph to the nearest 10 mph.

c The length of a leaf estimated at 8 cm to the nearest centimetre.

d The number of marbles in a bag estimated at 50 to the nearest 10 marbles.

e The number of marbles in a bag estimated at 50 to the nearest marble.

f The weight of some marbles in a bag estimated at 500 grams to the nearest 10 grams.

The four operations

Below are four calculations. Make up problems using the pictures that go with the four calculations.

   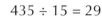

$70.9 \times 8 = 567.2$ $250 - 198 = 52$ $2.3 + 3.5 + 1.7 = 7.5$ $435 \div 15 = 29$

Example 9.3 ▷

a Find the product of 9 and 56.   **b** Find the remainder when 345 is divided by 51.

a   Product means 'multiply'. So, $9 \times 56 = 9 \times 50 + 9 \times 6 = 450 + 54 = 504$

b $345 \div 51 \approx 350 \div 50 = 7$. So, $7 \times 51 = 350 + 7 = 357$ which is too big.
$6 \times 51 = 306$, which gives $345 - 306 = 39$. The remainder is 39.

Example 9.4 ▷

A box of biscuits costs £1.99. How much will 28 boxes cost?

The easiest way to do this is: $28 \times £2$ minus 28p $= £56 - 28p = £55.72$.

Example 9.5 ▷

Mr Smith travels from Edinburgh (E) to Liverpool (L) and then to Bristol (B). Mr Jones travels directly from Edinburgh to Bristol. Use the distance chart to find out how much further Mr Smith travelled than Mr Jones.

Mr Smith travels $226 + 237 = 463$ miles. Mr Jones travels 383 miles.
$463 - 383 = 80$
So, Mr Smith travels 80 miles further.

	E	L	B
E		226	383
L	226		237
B	383	237	

Exercise 9B

1 How long does a train journey take if the train leaves at ten thirty-two am and arrives at one twelve pm?

2 Which mark is better: seventeen out of twenty or forty out of fifty?

3 How much does it cost to fill a 51-litre petrol tank at 80p per litre?

4 a A company has 197 boxes to move by van. The van can carry 23 boxes at a time. How many trips must the van make to move all the boxes?

b The same van does 34 miles to the gallon of petrol. Each trip above is 31 miles. Can the van deliver all the boxes if it has 8 gallons of petrol in the tank?

5 Find the sum and product of   **a** 5, 7 and 20   **b** 2, 38 and 50

6 Rajid has between 50 and 60 books. He arranged them in piles of four and found that he had one pile of three left over. He then arranged them in piles of five and found that he had one pile of four left over. How many books does Rajid have?

7 The local video shop is having a sale. Videos are £4.99 each or five for £20.

  a What is the cost of three videos?

  b What is the cost of ten videos?

  c What is the greatest number of video you can buy with £37?

8 **a** Three consecutive integers have a sum of 90. What are they?

  b Two consecutive integers have a product of 132. What are they?

  c Explain why there is more than one answer to this problem:
    Two consecutive integers have a difference of 1. What are they?

The magic number of this magic square is 50.

That means that the numbers in every row, in every column and in both diagonals add up to 50.

However, there are many more ways to make 50 by adding four numbers. For example, each of the following sets of 4 numbers makes 50.

5	18	11	16
12	15	6	17
14	9	20	7
19	8	13	10

5	18
12	15

5	16
19	10

18	11
8	13

How many more arrangements of four numbers can you find that add up to 50?

BODMAS

The following are instructions for making a cup of tea.

Can you put them in the right order?

Drink tea	Empty teapot	Fill kettle	Put milk in cup	Put teabag in teapot
Switch on kettle	Wait for tea to brew	Rinse teapot with hot water	Pour boiling water in teapot	Pour out tea

It is important that things are done in the right order. In mathematical operations there are rules about this.

The order of operations is called **BODMAS**, which stands for **B** (Brackets), **O** (Order or POwer), **D M** (Division and Multiplication) and **A S** (Addition and Subtraction).

Operations are always done in this order, which means that brackets are done first, followed by powers, then multiplication and division, and finally addition and subtraction.

Example 9.6 ▶

Circle the operation that you do first in each of these calculations. Then work out each one.

a $2 + 6 \div 2$ **b** $32 - 4 \times 5$ **c** $6 \div 3 - 1$ **d** $6 \div (3 - 1)$

a Division is done before addition, so you get $2 + 6 \div 2 = 2 + 3 = 5$
b Multiplication is done before subtraction, so you get $32 - 4 \times 5 = 32 - 20 = 12$
c Division is done before subtraction, so you get $6 \div 3 - 1 = 2 - 1 = 1$
d Brackets are done first, so you get $6 \div (3 - 1) = 6 \div 2 = 3$

Example 9.7 ▶

Work out each of the following, showing each step of the calculation.

a $1 + 3^2 \times 4 - 2$ **b** $(1 + 3)^2 \times (4 - 2)$

a The order will be power, multiplication, addition, subtraction (the last two can be interchanged). This gives
$$1 + 3^2 \times 4 - 2 = 1 + 9 \times 4 - 2 = 1 + 36 - 2 = 37 - 2 = 35$$
b The order will be brackets (both of them), power, multiplication. This gives
$$(1 + 3)^2 \times (4 - 2) = 4^2 \times 2 = 16 \times 2 = 32$$

Example 9.8 ▶

Put brackets into each of the following to make the calculation true.

a $5 + 1 \times 4 = 24$ **b** $1 + 3^2 - 4 = 12$ **c** $24 \div 6 - 2 = 6$

Decide which operation is done first.

a $(5 + 1) \times 4 = 24$

b $(1 + 3)^2 - 4 = 12$

c $24 \div (6 - 2) = 6$

Exercise 9C

1 Write down the operation that you do first in each of these calculations. Then work out each one.

   a $2 + 3 \times 6$ **b** $12 - 6 \div 3$ **c** $5 \times 5 + 2$ **d** $12 \div 4 - 2$
   e $(2 + 3) \times 6$ **f** $(12 - 3) \div 3$ **g** $5 \times (5 + 2)$ **h** $12 \div (4 - 2)$

2 Work out the following showing each step of the calculation.

   a $2 \times 3 + 4$ **b** $2 \times (3 + 4)$ **c** $2 + 3 \times 4$ **d** $(2 + 3) \times 4$
   e $4 \times 4 - 4$ **f** $5 + 3^2 + 6$ **g** $5 \times (3^2 + 6)$ **h** $3^2 - (5 - 2)$
   i $(2 + 3) \times (4 + 5)$ **j** $(2^2 + 3) \times (4 + 5)$ **k** $4 \div 4 + 4 \div 4$
   l $44 \div 4 + 4$ **m** $(6 + 2)^2$ **n** $6^2 + 2^2$ **o** $3^2 + 4 \times 6$

3 Put brackets into each of the following to make the calculation true.

   a $2 \times 5 + 4 = 18$ **b** $2 + 6 \times 3 = 24$ **c** $2 + 3 \times 1 + 6 = 35$
   d $5 + 2^2 \times 1 = 9$ **e** $3 + 2^2 = 25$ **f** $3 \times 4 + 3 + 7 = 28$
   g $3 + 4 \times 7 + 1 = 35$ **h** $3 + 4 \times 7 + 1 = 50$ **i** $9 - 5 - 2 = 6$
   j $9 - 5 \times 2 = 8$ **k** $4 + 4 + 4 \div 2 = 6$ **l** $1 + 4^2 - 9 - 2 = 18$

4 One of the calculations $2 \times 3^2 = 36$ and $2 \times 3^2 = 18$ is wrong. Which is it and how could you add brackets to make it true?

5 Work out the value of each of these.

a $(4 + 4) \div (4 + 4)$ b $(4 \times 4) \div (4 + 4)$ c $(4 + 4 + 4) \div 4$

d $4 \times (4 - 4) + 4$ e $(4 \times 4 + 4) \div 4$ f $(4 + 4 + 4) \div 2$

g $4 + 4 - 4 \div 4$ h $(4 + 4) \times (4 \div 4)$ i $(4 + 4) + 4 \div 4$

Extension Work

In Question 5, each calculation was made up of four 4s.

Work out the value of a $44 \div 4 - 4$ b $4 \times 4 - 4 \div 4$ c $4 \times 4 + 4 - 4$

Can you make other calculations using four 4s to give answers that you have not yet obtained in Question 5 or in the three calculations above?

Do as many as you can and see whether you can make all the values up to 20.

Repeat with five 5s. For example:

$(5 + 5) \div 5 - 5 \div 5 = 1$ $(5 \times 5 - 5) \div (5 + 5) = 2$

Long multiplication and long division

Example 9.9 ▶ Work out 36×43.

Below are four examples of the ways this calculation can be done. The answer is 1548.

Box method (partitioning)				Column method (expanded working)	Column method (compacted working)	Chinese method

Box method (partitioning)

×	30	6	
40	1200	240	1440
3	90	18	108
			1548

Column method (expanded working)

```
      36
  ×   43
      18  (3 × 6)
      90  (3 × 30)
     240  (40 × 6)
    1200  (40 × 30)
    1548
```

Column method (compacted working)

```
      36
  ×   43
     108  (3 × 36)
      1
    1440  (40 × 36)
    12
    1548
```

Chinese method

Example 9.10 ▶ Work out $543 \div 31$.

Below are two examples of the ways this can be done. The answer is 17, remainder 16.

Subtracting multiples

```
   543
 - 310  (10 × 31)
   233
 - 155  (5 × 31)
    78
 -  62  (2 × 31)
    16
```

Traditional method

```
        17
   31/543
        31
       233
       217
        16
```

1 Work out each of the following long multiplication problems. Use any method you are happy with.

a	17×23	**b**	32×42	**c**	19×45	**d**	56×46
e	12×346	**f**	32×541	**g**	27×147	**h**	39×213

2 Work out each of the following long division problems. Use any method you are happy with. Some of the problems will have a remainder.

a	$684 \div 19$	**b**	$966 \div 23$	**c**	$972 \div 36$	**d**	$625 \div 25$
e	$930 \div 38$	**f**	$642 \div 24$	**g**	$950 \div 33$	**h**	$800 \div 42$

Decide whether the following nine problems involve long multiplication or long division. Then do the appropriate calculation, showing your method clearly.

3 Each day 17 Jumbo jets fly from London to San Francisco. Each jet can carry up to 348 passengers. How many people can travel from London to San Francisco each day?

4 A company has 897 boxes to move by van. The van can carry 23 boxes at a time. How many trips must the van make to move all the boxes?

5 The same van does 34 miles to a gallon of petrol. How many miles can it do if the petrol tank holds 18 gallons?

6 The school photocopier can print 82 sheets a minute. If it runs without stopping for 45 minutes, how many sheets will it print?

7 The RE department has printed 525 sheets on Buddhism. These are put into folders in sets of 35. How many folders are there?

8 a To raise money, Wath Running Club are going to do a relay race from Wath to Edinburgh, which is 384 kilometres. Each runner will run 24 kilometres. How many runners will be needed to cover the distance?

b Sponsorship will bring in £32 per kilometre. How much money will the club raise?

9 Computer floppy disks are 45p each. How much will a box of 35 disks cost? Give your answer in pounds.

10 The daily newspaper sells advertising by the square inch. On Monday, it sells 232 square inches at £15 per square inch. How much money does it get from this advertising?

11 The local library has 13 000 books. Each shelf holds 52 books. How many shelves are there?

Another way of multiplying two two-digit numbers together is the 'Funny Face' method.

This shows how to do 26×57.

$$26 \times 57 = (20 + 6) \times (50 + 7)$$

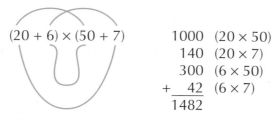

$(20 + 6) \times (50 + 7)$

1000	(20×50)
140	(20×7)
300	(6×50)
+ 42	(6×7)
1482	

Do a poster showing a calculation using the 'Funny Face' method.

Efficient calculations

You should have your own calculator, so that you can get used to it. Make sure that you understand how to use the basic functions ($\times$, $\div$, $+$, $-$) and the square, square root and brackets keys. They are different even on scientific calculators.

Example 9.11

Use a calculator to work out **a** $\dfrac{242 + 118}{88 - 72}$ **b** $\dfrac{63 \times 224}{32 \times 36}$

The line that separates the top numbers from the bottom numbers acts both as a divide sign ($\div$) and as brackets.

a Key the calculation as $(242 + 118) \div (88 - 72) = 22.5$

b Key the calculation as $(63 \times 224) \div (32 \times 36) = 12.25$

Example 9.12

Use a calculator to work out **a** $\sqrt{1764}$ **b** 23.4^2 **c** $52.3 - (30.4 - 17.3)$

a Some calculators need the square root after the number has been keyed, some need it before: $\sqrt{1764} = 42$

b Most calculators have a special key for squaring: $23.4^2 = 547.56$

c This can be keyed in exactly as it reads: $52.3 - (30.4 - 17.3) = 39.2$

Exercise 9E

1 Without using a calculator, work out the value of each of these.

a $\dfrac{17 + 8}{7 - 2}$ **b** $\dfrac{53 - 8}{3.5 - 2}$ **c** $\dfrac{19.2 - 1.7}{5.6 - 3.1}$

2 Use a calculator to do the calculations in Question 1. Do you get the same answers?

For each part, write down the sequence of keys that you pressed to get the answer.

3 Work out the value of each of these. Round off your answers to 1 dp.

a $\dfrac{194 + 866}{122 + 90}$ b $\dfrac{213 + 73}{63 - 19}$ c $\dfrac{132 + 88}{78 - 28}$ d $\dfrac{792 + 88}{54 - 21}$

e $\dfrac{790 \times 84}{24 \times 28}$ f $\dfrac{642 \times 24}{87 - 15}$ g $\dfrac{107 + 853}{24 \times 16}$ h $\dfrac{57 - 23}{18 - 7.8}$

4 Estimate the answer to $\dfrac{231 + 167}{78 - 32}$

Now use a calculator to work out the answer to 1 dp. Is it about the same?

5 Work out each of these.

a $\sqrt{42.25}$ b $\sqrt{68.89}$ c 2.6^2 d 3.9^2

e $\sqrt{(23.8 + 66.45)}$ f $\sqrt{(7 - 5.04)}$ g $(5.2 - 1.8)^2$ h $(2.5 + 6.1)^2$

6 Work out

a $8.3 - (4.2 - 1.9)$ b $12.3 + (3.2 - 1.7)^2$ c $(3.2 + 1.9)^2 - (5.2 - 2.1)^2$

7 Use a calculator to find the quotient and the remainder when

a 985 is divided by 23 b 802 is divided by 36

8 A calculator shows an answer of

2.33333333333

Write this as a mixed number or a top heavy fraction.

Extension Work

Time calculations are difficult to do on a calculator as there are not 100 minutes in an hour. So, you need to know either the decimal equivalents of all the divisions of an hour or the way to work them out. For example: 15 minutes is 0.25 of an hour.

Copy and complete this table for some of the decimal equivalents to fractions of an hour.

Time (min)	5	6	12	15	20	30	40	45	54	55
Fraction	$\frac{1}{12}$	$\frac{1}{10}$		$\frac{1}{4}$	$\frac{1}{3}$				$\frac{9}{10}$	
Decimal	0.166		0.2	0.25			0.667			0.917

When a time is given as a decimal and it is not one of those in the table above, you need a way to work it out in hours and minutes. For example:

3.4578 hours: subtract 3 to give 0.4578, then multiply by 60 to give 27.468

This is 27 minutes to the nearest minute. So, 3.4578 ≈ 3 hours 27 minutes.

1 Find each of the following decimal times as a time in hours and minutes.

a 2.5 h b 3.25 h c 4.75 h d 3.1 h

e 4.6 h f 3.3333 h g 1.15 h h 4.3 h

i 0.45 h j 0.95 h k 3.666 h

2 Find each of the following times in hours and minutes as a decimal time.

a 2 h 40 min b 1 h 45 min c 2 h 18 min d 1 h 20 min

Calculating with measurements

The following table shows the relationship between the common metric units.

1000	100	10	1	0.1	0.01	0.001
km			m		cm	mm
kg			g			mg
			l		cl	ml

Example 9.13 ▷

Add together 1.23 m, 46 cm and 0.034 km.

First convert all the lengths to the same unit.

1000	100	10	1	0.1	0.01	0.001
km			m		cm	mm
			1	2	3	
				4	6	
0	0	3	4			

The answer is 0.035 69 km or 35.69 m or 3569 cm. 35.69 m is the sensible answer.

Example 9.14 ▷

A recipe needs 550 grams of flour to make a cake. How many 1 kg bags of flour will be needed to make six cakes?

Six cakes will need $6 \times 550 = 3300$ g, which will need four bags of flour.

Example 9.15 ▷

What unit would you use to measure each of these?

a   Width of a football field

b   Length of a pencil

c   Weight of a car

d   Spoonful of medicine

Choose a sensible unit. Sometimes there is more than one answer.

a   Metre   b   Centimetre   c   Kilogram   d   Millilitre

Example 9.16 ▷

Convert   a   6 cm to mm   b   1250 g to kg   c   5 l to cl

You need to know the conversion factors.

a   1 cm = 10 mm: $6 \times 10 = 60$ mm

b   1000 g = 1 kg: $1250 \div 1000 = 1.25$ kg

c   1 l = 100 cl: 5 l = $5 \times 100 = 500$ cl

1 Convert each of the following lengths to centimetres.

    a 60 mm   **b** 2 m   **c** 743 mm   **d** 0.007 km   **e** 12.35 m

2 Convert each of the following lengths to kilometres.

    a 456 m   **b** 7645 m   **c** 6532 cm   **d** 21 358 mm   **e** 54 m

3 Convert each of the following lengths to millimetres.

    a 34 cm   **b** 3 m   **c** 3 km   **d** 35.6 cm   **e** 0.7 cm

4 Convert each of the following masses to kilograms.

    a 3459 g   **b** 215 g   **c** 65 120 g   **d** 21 g   **e** 210 g

5 Convert each of the following masses to grams.

    a 4 kg   **b** 4.32 kg   **c** 0.56 kg   **d** 0.007 kg   **e** 6.784 kg

6 Convert each of the following capacities to litres.

    a 237 cl   **b** 3097 ml   **c** 1862 cl   **d** 48 cl   **e** 96 427 ml

7 Convert each of the following times to hours and minutes.

    a 70 min   **b** 125 min   **c** 87 min   **d** 200 min   **e** 90 min

8 Add together each of the following groups of measurements and give the answer in an appropriate unit.

    a 1.78 m, 39 cm, 0.006 km   **b** 0.234 kg, 60 g, 0.004 kg

    c 2.3 l, 46 cl, 726 ml   **d** 0.000 6 km, 23 mm, 3.5 cm

9 Fill in each missing unit.

    a A two-storey house is about 7…… high   **b** John weighs about 47……

    c Mary lives about 2…… from school   **d** Ravid ran a marathon in 3……

10 Read the value from each of the following scales.

    a   **b**   **c**

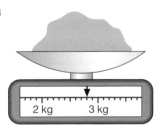

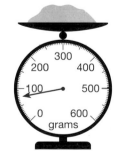

d   **e**   **f**

   0   50   200   100   0   20

LEVEL 5

4 *1996 Paper 1*

Gwen makes kites to sell. She sells the kites for £4.75 each.

a Gwen sells 26 kites. How much does she get for the 26 kites?

b Gwen has a box of 250 staples. She uses 16 staples to make each kite.

How many complete kites can she make using the 250 staples?

5 *1997 Paper 1*

a A shop sells plants at 95p each. Find the cost of 35 plants.

b The shop also sells trees at £17 each. Mr Bailey has £250. He wants to buy as many trees as possible.

How many trees can Mr Bailey buy?

6 *1999 Paper 2*

This formula tells you how tall a boy is likely to be when he grows up.

> Add the mother's and father's heights.
> Divide by 2.
> Add 7 cm to the result.
> The boy is likely to be this height, plus or minus 10 cm.

Marc's mother is 168 cm tall. His father is 194 cm tall. What is the greatest height Marc is likely to be when he grows up?

7 *2000 Paper 2*

a A club wants to take 3000 people on a journey to London using coaches. Each coach can carry 52 people. How many coaches do they need?

b Each coach costs £420. What is the total cost of the coaches?

c How much is each person's share of the cost?

This chapter is going to show you

- what square numbers and triangle numbers are
- how to draw graphs from functions
- how to use algebra to solve problems
- how to use a calculator to find square roots

What you should already know

- How to find the term-to-term rule in a sequence
- How to plot coordinates
- How to solve simple equations

Square numbers and square roots

When we multiply any number by itself, the answer is called the **square of the number** or the **number squared**. We call this operation **squaring**. We show it by putting a small 2 at the top right-hand corner of the number being squared. For example:

$$4 \times 4 = 4^2 = 16$$

The result of squaring a number is also called a **square number**. The first ten square numbers are shown below.

1×1	2×2	3×3	4×4	5×5	6×6	7×7	8×8	9×9	10×10
1^2	2^2	3^2	4^2	5^2	6^2	7^2	8^2	9^2	10^2
1	4	9	16	25	36	49	64	81	100

You need to learn all of these.

The **square root** of a number is that number which, when squared, gives the starting number. It is the opposite of finding the square of a number. We represent a square root by the symbol $\sqrt{}$. For example:

$$\sqrt{1} = 1 \qquad \sqrt{4} = 2 \qquad \sqrt{9} = 3 \qquad \sqrt{16} = 4 \qquad \sqrt{25} = 5$$

Only the square root of a square number will give an integer (whole number) as the answer.

Exercise 10A

1 Look at the pattern on the right.

a Copy this pattern and draw the next two shapes in the pattern.

b What is special about the total number of dots in each pattern number?

c What is special about the number of blue dots in each pattern number?

d What is special about the number of red dots in each pattern number?

e Write down a connection between square numbers and odd numbers.

Pattern 1

1

Pattern 2

1 + 3
4

Pattern 3

4 + 5
9

See also the graphs of $y = 2$ and $y = 5$, shown below.

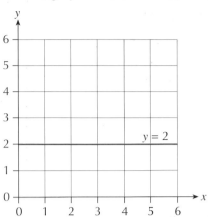 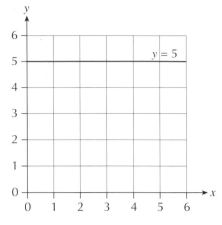

Note: the graphs are always horizontal lines for $y = A$, where A is any fixed number.

When we repeat this for an x-value, say $x = 2$, we get a vertical line, as shown.

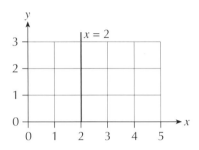

Exercise 10D

1 a Draw the following graphs on the same grid, and label them.

     i $y = 1$ **ii** $y = 4$ **iii** $y = 6$

     iv $x = 1$ **v** $x = 3$ **vi** $x = 5$

> **Axes**
> x-axis from 0 to 7
> y-axis from 0 to 7

b Write the coordinates of the point where each pair of lines cross.

     i $y = 1$ and $x = 3$ **ii** $y = 4$ and $x = 1$ **iii** $y = 6$ and $x = 5$

2 a For each of the equations in the box below, copy and complete the arrow diagram and the set of coordinates.

Start your arrow diagram as follows:

$x \longrightarrow ?$	**Coordinates**		
$0 \longrightarrow$	$(0, \ \ )$		$y = x$
$1 \longrightarrow$	$(1, \ \ )$		$y = 2x$
$2 \longrightarrow$	$(2, \ \ )$		$y = 3x$
$3 \longrightarrow$	$(3, \ \ )$		$y = 4x$
$4 \longrightarrow$	$(4, \ \ )$		$y = 5x$
$5 \longrightarrow$	$(5, \ \ )$		

b For each set of coordinates, draw a graph on the same pair of axes as those for the other equations. Not all your points will fit on the grid, so plot the points that will fit on, and join them.

> **Axes**
> x-axis from 0 to 5
> y-axis from 0 to 12

c Explain what you notice.

d Try putting the graph of $y = 7x$ on your diagram without calculating the coordinates.

a For each of the equations in the box below, copy and complete the arrow diagram and the set of coordinates.

Start your arrow diagram as follows:

$x \longrightarrow$?	**Coordinates**
$0 \longrightarrow$	$(0, \ )$
$1 \longrightarrow$	$(1, \ )$
$2 \longrightarrow$	$(2, \ )$
$3 \longrightarrow$	$(3, \ )$
$4 \longrightarrow$	$(4, \ )$
$5 \longrightarrow$	$(5, \ )$

$y = x$

$y = x + 1$

$y = x + 2$

$y = x + 3$

$y = x + 4$

b For each set of coordinates, draw a graph on the same pair of axes as those for the other equations. Not all your points will fit on the grid, so plot the points that will fit on, and join them.

Axes
x-axis from 0 to 5
y-axis from 0 to 10

c Explain what you notice.

d Try putting the graph of $y = x + 5$ on your diagram.

Extension Work

1 Use a spreadsheet to draw the graph of $y = 2x + 3$.

2 Use a graphics calculator to draw all the graphs in Exercise 10D.

Questions about graphs

Example 10.1 ▷

Which of the points (2, 5) and (3, 9) are on the graph of $y = 2x + 3$?

Look at (2, 5). When $x = 2$:

$y = 2x + 3 = 2 \times 2 + 3 = 7$ (which is not 5)

So, the point (2, 5) is not on the line $y = 2x + 3$.

Look at (3, 9). When $x = 3$:

$y = 2x + 3 = 2 \times 3 + 3 = 9$

So, the point (3, 9) is on the line $y = 2x + 3$.

You can check this by looking on the graph of $y = 2x + 3$.

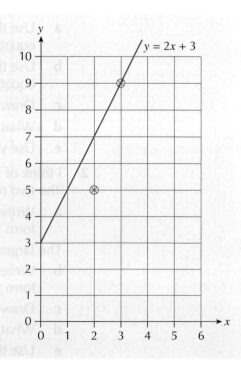

Estimating angles

● Copy the table below.

Angle	Estimate	Actual	Difference
1			
2			
3			
4			

● Estimate the size of each of the four angles below and complete the Estimate column in the table.

1 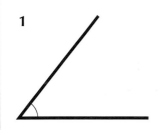   2    3 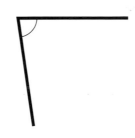   4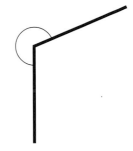

● Now measure the size of each angle to the nearest degree and complete the Actual column.
● Work out the difference between your estimate and the actual measurement for each angle and complete the Difference column.

Constructions

You need to be able to draw a shape exactly from information given on a diagram, using a ruler and a protractor. This is known as **constructing a shape**.

When constructing a shape you need to draw lines to the nearest millimetre and the angles to the nearest degree.

Example 11.3 ▶

Construct the triangle ABC.
● Draw line BC 7.5 cm long.
● Draw an angle of 50° at B.
● Draw line AB 4.1 cm long.
● Join AC to complete the triangle.

The completed, full-sized triangle is given below.

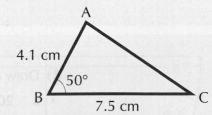

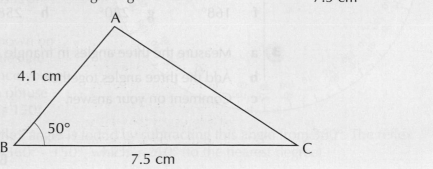

Example 11.4 ▶

Construct the triangle XYZ.
- Draw line YZ 8.3 cm long.
- Draw an angle of 42° at Y.
- Draw an angle of 51° at Z.
- Extend both angle lines to intersect at X to complete the triangle.

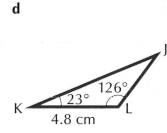

The completed, full-sized triangle is given below.

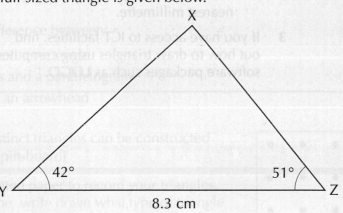

Exercise 11B

① Construct each of the following triangles. Remember to label all lines and angles.

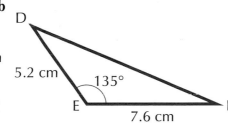

a
A, 6.2 cm, 58°, B, 5.6 cm, C

b
D, 5.2 cm, 135°, E, 7.6 cm, F

c
G, 44°, 67°, H, 6.8 cm, I

d
J, 126°, 23°, K, 4.8 cm, L

② a Construct the triangle PQR.
b Measure the size of ∠P and ∠R to the nearest degree.
c Measure the length of the line PR to the nearest millimetre.

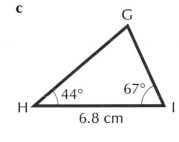

③ Construct the triangle ABC with ∠A = 100°, ∠B = 36° and AB = 8.4 cm.

④ a Construct the trapezium ABCD.
b Measure the size of ∠B to the nearest degree.
c Measure the length of the lines AB and BC to the nearest millimetre.

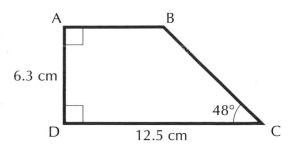

<table>
<tr><td>

This chapter is going to show you

o how to find simple percentages and use them to compare proportions

o how to work out ratio, leading into simple direct proportion

o how to solve problems using ratio

</td><td>

What you should already know

o How to find equivalent fractions, percentages and decimals

o How to find multiples of 10% of a quantity

o Division facts from tables up to 10 × 10

</td></tr>
</table>

Percentages

One of these labels is from a packet of porridge oats. The other is from a toffee cake.

Compare the percentages of protein, carbohydrates, fat and fibre.

PORRIDGE OATS	
Typical values	**per 100 g**
Energy	1555 kJ/ 372 kcal
Protein	7.5 g
Carbohydrates	71 g
Fat	6.0 g
Fibre	6.0 g
Sodium	0.3 g

TOFFEE CAKE	
Typical values	**per 100 g**
Energy	1421 kJ/ 340 kcal
Protein	2.9 g
Carbohydrates	39.1 g
Fat	19.1 g
Fibre	0.3 g
Sodium	0.2 g

Example 12.1 ▷

Without using a calculator find   **a**   12% of £260   **b**   39% of 32

a   12% = 10% + 1% + 1% = 26 + 2.6 + 2.6 = £31.20

b   39% = 10% + 10% + 10% + 10% − 1% = 4 × 3.2 − 0.32 = 12.8 − 0.32 = 12.48

Example 12.2 ▷

Work out   **a**   6% of £190   **b**   63% of 75 eggs

a   (6 ÷ 100) × 190 = £11.40

b   (63 ÷ 100) × 75 = 47.25 = 47 eggs

Example 12.3 ▷

Which is greater, 42% of 560 or 62% of 390?

(42 ÷ 100) × 560 = 235.2   (62 ÷ 100) × 390 = 241.8

62% of 390 is greater.

1 Write down or work out the equivalent percentage and decimal to each of these fractions.

   a $\frac{2}{5}$ **b** $\frac{1}{4}$ **c** $\frac{3}{8}$ **d** $\frac{11}{20}$ **e** $\frac{21}{25}$

2 Write down or work out the equivalent percentage and fraction to each of these decimals.

   a 0.1   **b** 0.75   **c** 0.34   **d** 0.85   **e** 0.31

3 Write down or work out the equivalent fraction and decimal to each of these percentages.

   a 15%   **b** 62.5%   **c** 8%   **d** 66.6%   **e** 80%

4 Without using a calculator, work out each of these.

   a 12% of 320   **b** 49% of 45   **c** 31% of 260   **d** 18% of 68

   e 11% of 12   **f** 28% of 280   **g** 52% of 36   **h** 99% of 206

5 Work out each of these.

   a 13% of £560   **b** 46% of 64 books   **c** 73% of 190 chairs

   d 34% of £212   **e** 64% of 996 pupils   **f** 57% of 120 buses

   g 37% of 109 plants   **h** 78% of 345 bottles   **i** 62% of 365 days

   j 93% of 2564 people   **k** 54% of 456 fish   **l** 45% of £45

   m 65% of 366 eggs   **n** 7% of £684   **o** 9% of 568 chickens

6 Which is bigger:

   a 45% of 68 or 34% of 92?   **b** 22% of £86 or 82% of £26?

   c 28% of 79 or 69% of 31?   **d** 32% of 435 or 43% of 325?

7 Javid scores 17 out of 25 on a maths test, 14 out of 20 on a science test and 33 out of 50 on an English test. Work out each score as a percentage.

8 Arrange these numbers in order of increasing size.

   a 21%, $\frac{6}{25}$, 0.2   **b** 0.39, 38%, $\frac{3}{8}$ **c** $\frac{11}{20}$, 54%, 0.53

Extension Work

The pie chart shows the percentage of each constituent of the toffee cake given in the label on page 124.

Draw a pie chart to show the percentage of each constituent of the porridge oats given on the same page.

Obtain labels from a variety of cereals and other food items. Draw a pie chart for each of them.

What types of food have the most fat? What types of food have the most energy?

Is there a connection between the energy of food and the fat and carbohydrate content?

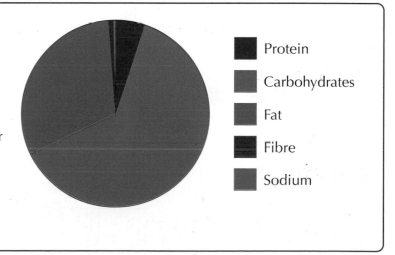

Protein

Carbohydrates

Fat

Fibre

Sodium

Ratio and proportion

Look at the fish tank. There are three types of fish – plain, striped and spotted.

What proportion of the fish are plain? What proportion are striped? What proportion are spotted?

What is the ratio of plain fish to striped fish?

What is the ratio of striped fish to spotted fish?

What is the ratio of plain fish to striped fish?

Proportion is a way of comparing the parts of a quantity to the whole quantity.

Example 12.4 ▷ What proportion of this metre rule is shaded? What is the ratio of the shaded part to the unshaded part?

40 cm out of 100 cm are shaded. This is 40% (or 0.4 or $\frac{2}{5}$).The ratio of shaded to unshaded is $40:60 = 2:3$.

Example 12.5 ▷ A fruit drink is made by mixing 20 cl of orange juice with 60 cl of pineapple juice. What is the proportion of orange juice in the drink?

Total volume of drink is $20 + 60 = 80$ cl

The proportion of orange is 20 out of $80 = \frac{20}{80} = \frac{1}{4}$

Example 12.6 ▷ Another fruit drink is made by mixing orange juice and grapefruit juice. The proportion of orange is 40%. 60 cl of orange juice is used. What proportion of grapefruit is used? How much grapefruit juice is used?

The proportion of grapefruit is $100\% - 40\% = 60\%$. Now $40\% = 60$ cl, so $10\% = 15$ cl. Hence, $60\% = 90$ cl of grapefruit juice.

Example 12.7 ▷ Five pens cost £3.25. How much do 8 pens cost?

First, work out cost of 1 pen: £3.25 ÷ 5 = £0.65
Hence, 8 pens cost 8 × £0.65 = £5.20

Exercise 12B

1 For each of these metre rules:
   i   What proportion of the rule is shaded?
   ii What is the ratio of the shaded part to the unshaded part?

   a
   b
   c
   d

2 For each bag of black and white balls:

   i What proportion of the balls are black?

   ii What is the ratio of black to white balls?

   a   **b**   **c**   **d**

3 Tom and Jerry have some coins. This table shows the coins they have.

	1p	2p	5p	10p	20p	50p
Tom	15	45	50	80	20	40
Jerry	18	36	72	24	20	30

   a How much do they each have altogether?

   b How many coins do they each have?

   c Copy and complete the table below, which shows the proportion of each coin that they have.

	1p	2p	5p	10p	20p	50p
Tom	6%	18%				
Jerry						

   d Add up the proportions for Tom and for Jerry. Explain your answer.

4 Three bars of soap cost £1.80. How much would   **a** 12 bars cost?   **b** 30 bars cost?

5 One litre of fruit squash contains 24 cl of fruit concentrate and the rest is water.

   a What proportion of the drink is fruit concentrate?

   b What proportion of the drink is water?

6 One euro is worth £0.62. How many pounds will I get for each of the following numbers of euros?

   a 5 euros   **b** 8 euros   **c** 600 euros.

7 These are the ingredients to make four pancakes.

   a How much of each ingredient will be needed to make 12 pancakes?

   b How much of each ingredient will be needed to make six pancakes?

> 1 egg
> 3 ounces of plain flour
> 5 fluid ounces of milk

8 The ratio of British cars to foreign cars in the staff car park is 1 : 4. Explain why the proportion of British cars is 20% and not 25%.

Solving problems

A painter has a 5-litre can of blue paint and 3 litres of yellow paint in a 5-litre can (Picture 1).

Picture 1   **Picture 2**   **Picture 3**

He pours 2 litres of blue paint into the other can (Picture 2) and mixes it thoroughly.

He then pours 1 litre from the second can back into the first can (Picture 3) and mixes it thoroughly.

How much blue paint is in the first can now?

Example 12.11 ▷ | Divide £150 in the ratio 1:5.
|
| There are 1 + 5 = 6 portions. This gives £150 ÷ 6 = £25 per portion. So one share of the £150 is 1 × 25 = £25, and the other share is 5 × £25 = £125.

Example 12.12 ▷ | Two-fifths of a packet of bulbs are daffodils. The rest are tulips. What is the ratio of daffodils to tulips?
|
| Ratio is $\frac{2}{5} : \frac{3}{5} = 2:3$

Exercise 12D

1. Divide £100 in the ratio

   a 2:3   **b** 1:9   **c** 3:7   **d** 1:3   **e** 9:11

2. There are 350 pupils in a primary school. The ratio of girls to boys is 3:2. How many boys and girls are there in the school?

3. Freda has 120 CDs. The ratio of pop CDs to dance CDs is 5:7. How many of each type of CD are there?

4. James is saving 50p coins and £1 coins. He has 75 coins. The ratio of 50p coins to £1 coins is 7:8. How much money does he have altogether?

5. Mr Smith has 24 calculators in a box. The ratio of ordinary calculators to scientific calculators is 5:1. How many of each type of calculator does he have?

6. An exam consists of three parts. A mental test, a non-calculator paper and a calculator paper. The ratio of marks for each is 1:3:4. The whole exam is worth 120 marks. How many marks does each part of the exam get?

7. **a** There are 15 bottles on the wall. The ratio of green bottles to brown bottles is 1:4. How many green bottles are there on the wall?

   b One green bottle accidentally falls. What is the ratio of green to brown bottles now?

8 **a** Forty-nine trains pass through Barnsley station each day. They go to Huddersfield or Leeds in the ratio 3 : 4. How many trains go to Huddersfield?

b One day, due to driver shortages, six of the Huddersfield trains are cancelled and three of the Leeds trains are cancelled. What is the ratio of Huddersfield trains to Leeds trains that day?

Uncle Fred has decided to give his nephew and niece, Jack and Jill, £100 between them. He decides to split the £100 in the ratio of their ages. Jack is 4 and Jill is 6.

a How much do each get?

b The following year he does the same thing with another £100. How much do each get now?

c He continues to give them £100 shared in the ratio of their ages for another 8 years. How much will each get each year?

d After the 10 years, how much of the £1000 given in total will Jack have? How much will Jill have?

What you need to know for level 4

- How to work out simple fractions
- How to work out simple percentages
- Recognise simple proportions of a whole

What you need to know for level 5

- How to solve simple problems using ratio and direct proportion
- The link between a proportion and the equivalent decimal, fraction and percentage

National Curriculum SATs questions

LEVEL 4

1 *1998 Paper 1*

Here are the ingredients for 1 fruit cake.

1 fruit cake	10 fruit cakes
200 g self-raising flour	2000 g = 2 kg self-raising flour
100 g caster sugar	...... g = ... kg caster sugar
150 g margarine	...... g = ... kg margarine
125 g mixed fruit	...... g = ... kg mixed fruit
3 eggs	30 eggs

a Copy and complete the table to show how much of each ingredient you need to make 10 fruit cakes.

b 6 eggs cost 70p. How much will 30 eggs cost?

Rotational symmetry

A 2-D shape has **rotational symmetry** when it can be rotated about a point to look exactly the same in a new position.

The **order of rotational symmetry** is the number of different positions in which the shape looks the same when it is rotated about the point through one complete turn (360°).

A shape has no rotational symmetry when it has to be rotated through one complete turn to look exactly the same. So it is said to have rotational symmetry of order 1.

To find the order of rotational symmetry of a shape, use tracing paper.

- First, trace the shape.
- Then rotate the tracing paper until the tracing again fits exactly over the shape.
- Count the number the times that the tracing fits exactly over the shape until you return to the starting position.
- The number of times that the tracing fits is the order of rotational symmetry.

Example 14.4 ▷ This shape has rotational symmetry of order 3.

Example 14.5 ▷ This shape has rotational symmetry of order 4.

Example 14.6 ▷ This shape has no rotational symmetry.
Therefore, it has rotational symmetry of order 1.

Exercise 14B

1 Copy each of these capital letters and write below its order of rotational symmetry.

a **H** b **M** c **N** d **S** e **W** f **X**

2 Write down the order of rotational symmetry for each of the shapes below.

a b c d e f

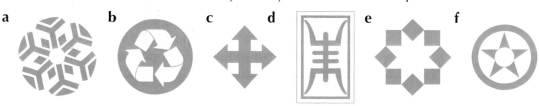

3 Copy and complete the table for each of the following regular polygons.

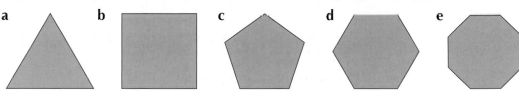

a   b   c   d   e

	Shape	Number of lines of symmetry	Order of rotational symmetry
a	Equilateral triangle		
b	Square		
c	Regular pentagon		
d	Regular hexagon		
e	Regular octagon		

What do you notice?

Extension Work

a   Make eight copies of this shape on square dotty paper.

b   Cut them out and arrange them to make a pattern with rotational symmetry of order 8.

c   Design your own pattern which has rotational symmetry of order 8.

Reflections

The picture shows an L-shape reflected in a mirror.

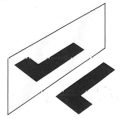

You can draw the picture without the mirror, as follows?

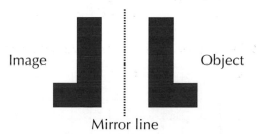

Image   Object

Mirror line

The **object** is reflected in the mirror line to give the **image**. The mirror line becomes a line of symmetry. So, if the paper is folded along the mirror line, the object will fit exactly over the image. The image is the same distance from the mirror line as the object.

A reflection is an example of a **transformation**. A transformation is a way of changing the position or the size of a shape.

Example 14.7 ▷ Reflect this shape in the given mirror line.

Notice that the image is the same size as the object, and that the mirror line becomes a line of symmetry.

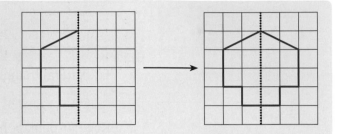

Example 14.8 ▷ Triangle A′B′C′ is the reflection of triangle ABC in the given mirror line.

When we change the position of a shape, we sometimes use the term **map**. Here we could write:

△ABC is mapped onto △A′B′C′ by a reflection in the mirror line.

Notice that the line joining A to A′ is perpendicular to the mirror line. This is true for all corresponding points on the object and the image. Also, all corresponding points on the object and image are at the same perpendicular distance from the mirror line.

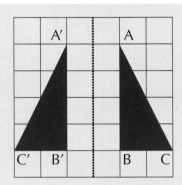

Example 14.9 ▷ Reflect this rectangle in the mirror line shown.

Use tracing paper to check the reflection.

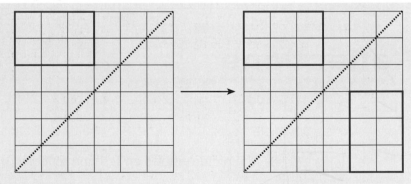

Exercise 14C ① Copy each of these diagrams onto squared paper and draw its reflection in the given mirror line.

a
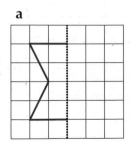

b
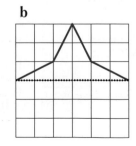

c
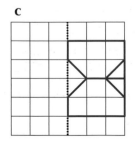

d
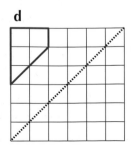

2 Copy each of these shapes onto squared paper and draw its reflection in the given mirror line.

a 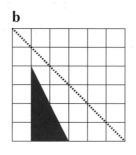   b 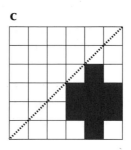   c 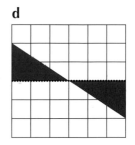   d

3 The points A(1, 2), B(2, 5), C(4, 4) and D(6, 1) are shown on the grid.

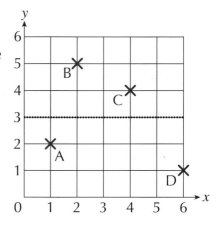

  a   Copy the grid onto squared paper and plot the points A, B, C and D. Draw the mirror line.

  b   Reflect the points in the mirror line and label them A′, B′, C′ and D′.

  c   Write down the coordinates of the image points.

  d   The point E(12, 6) is mapped onto E′ by a reflection in the mirror line. What are the coordinates of E′?

Extension Work

1 **a** Copy the diagram onto squared paper and reflect the triangle in the series of parallel mirrors.

  b   Make up your own patterns using a series of parallel mirrors.

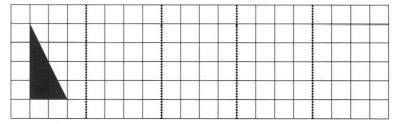

2 **a** Copy the grid onto squared paper and draw the triangle ABC. Write down the coordinates of A, B and C.

  b   Reflect the triangle in the *x*-axis. Label the vertices of the image A′, B′ and C′. What are the coordinates of A′, B′ and C′?

  c   Reflect triangle A′B′C′ in the *y*-axis. Label the vertices of this image A″, B″ and C″. What are the coordinates of A″, B″ and C″?

  d   Reflect triangle A″B″C″ in the *x*-axis. Label the vertices A‴, B‴ and C‴. What are the coordinates of A‴B‴C‴.

  e   Describe the reflection that maps triangle A″B″C″ onto triangle ABC.

3 Use ICT software, such as Logo, to reflect shapes in mirror lines.

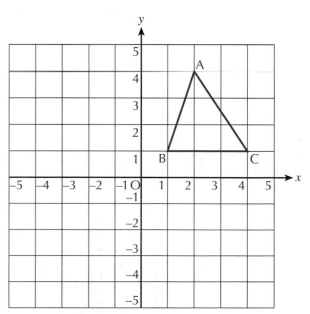

Rotations

Another type of transformation in geometry is **rotation**.

To describe the rotation of a 2-D shape, three facts must be known:
- **Centre of rotation** – the point about which the shape rotates.
- **Angle of rotation** – this is usually 90° ($\frac{1}{4}$ turn), 180° ($\frac{1}{2}$ turn) or 270° ($\frac{3}{4}$ turn).
- **Direction of rotation** – clockwise or anticlockwise.

When you rotate a shape, it is a good idea to use tracing paper.

As with reflections, the original shape is called the object, and the rotated shape is called the image.

Example 14.10 ▶

The flag is rotated through 90° clockwise about the point X.

Notice that this is the same as rotating the flag through 270° anticlockwise about the point X.

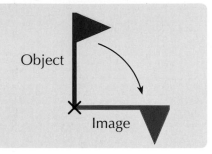

Example 14.11 ▶

This right-angled triangle is rotated through 180° clockwise about the point X.

Notice that this triangle can be rotated either clockwise or anticlockwise when turning through 180°.

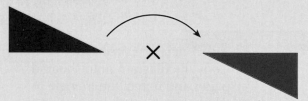

Example 14.12 ▶

△ABC has been mapped onto △A'B'C' by a rotation of 90° anticlockwise about the point X.

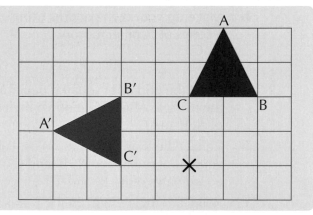

Exercise 14D

1. Copy each of the flags below and draw the image after each one has been rotated about the point marked X through the angle indicated. Use tracing paper to help.

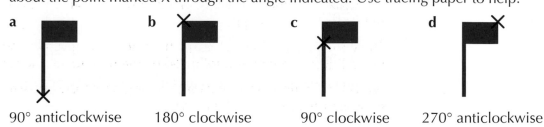

a   90° anticlockwise   b   180° clockwise   c   90° clockwise   d   270° anticlockwise

2 Copy each of the shapes below onto a square grid. Draw the image after each one has been rotated about the point marked X through the angle indicated. Use tracing paper to help.

a

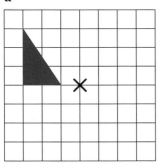

180° clockwise

b

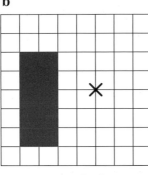

90° anticlockwise

c

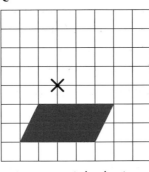

180° anticlockwise

d

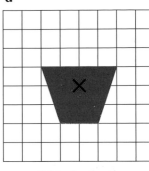

90° clockwise

3 **a** Rotate the rectangle ABCD through 90° clockwise about the point (1,2) to give the image A'B'C'D'.

b Write down the coordinates of A', B', C' and D'.

c Which coordinate point remains fixed throughout the rotation?

d What rotation will map the rectangle A'B'C'D' onto the rectangle ABCD?

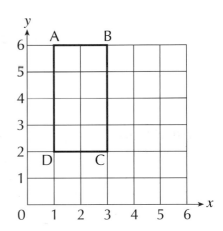

Extension Work

1 **Inverse rotations**

The **inverse** of a rotation is that rotation required to map the image back onto the object, using the same centre of rotation. Investigate inverse rotations by drawing your own shapes and using different rotations.

Write down any properties you discover about inverse rotations.

2 Use ICT software, such as Logo, to rotate shapes about different centres of rotation.

Translations

A translation is the movement of a 2-D shape from one position to another without reflecting it or rotating it.

The distance and direction of the translation are given by the number of unit squares moved to the right or left, followed by the number of unit squares moved up or down.

As with reflections and rotations, the original shape is called the object, and the translated shape is called the image.

Example 14.13 ▶ Triangle A has been mapped onto triangle B by a translation 3 units right, followed by 2 units up.

Points on triangle A are mapped by the same translation onto triangle B, as shown by the arrows.

When an object is translated onto its image, every point on the object moves the same distance.

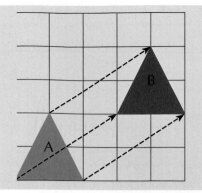

Example 14.14 ▶ The rectangle ABCD has been mapped onto rectangle A'B'C'D' by a translation 3 units left, followed by 3 units down.

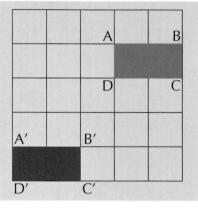

Exercise 14E

1 Describe each of the following translations:

   a from A to B

   b from A to C

   c from A to D

   d from A to E

   e from B to D

   f from C to E

   g from D to E

   h from E to A

2 Copy the triangle ABC onto squared paper. Label it P.

   a Write down the coordinates of the vertices of triangle P.

   b Translate triangle P 6 units left and 2 units down. Label the new triangle Q.

   c Write down the coordinates of the vertices of triangle Q.

   d Translate triangle Q 5 units right and 4 units down. Label the new triangle R.

   e Write down the coordinates of the vertices of triangle R.

   f Describe the translation which maps triangle R onto triangle P.

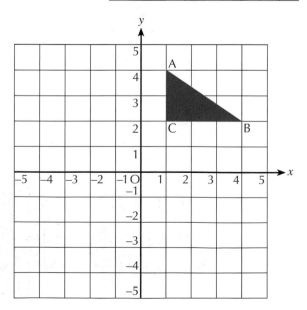

Use squared dotty paper or a pin-board for this investigation.

a How many different translations of the triangle are possible on this 3 by 3 grid?

b How many different translations of this triangle are possible on a 4 by 4 grid?

c Investigate the number of translations that are possible on any size grid.

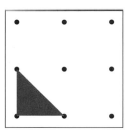

What you need to know for level 4

- How to find the order of rotational symmetry of a shape
- How to reflect simple shapes in a mirror line

What you need to know for level 5

- Be able to recognise and visualise transformations of 2-D shapes:
  - reflections
  - rotations
  - translations

National Curriculum SATs questions

LEVEL 4

1 *1998 Paper 1*

These patterns are from Islamic designs. Write down the number of lines of symmetry for each pattern.

a

b

c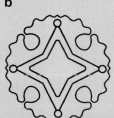

2 *1995 Paper 2*

These patterns come from Egypt. Write down the order of rotational symmetry for each one.

a

b

c

d

LEVEL 5

3 *1999 Paper 2*

a Copy the diagram onto squared paper. You can rotate triangle A onto triangle B.

Put a cross on the centre of rotation. You may use tracing paper to help you.

b You can rotate triangle A onto triangle B. The rotation is anti-clockwise. What is the angle of rotation?

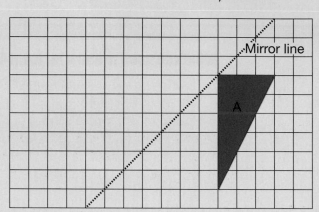

c Copy the diagram onto squared paper. Reflect triangle A in the mirror line. You may use a mirror or tracing paper to help you.

4 *1999 Paper 1*

Write the letter of each shape in the correct space in the table below. You may use a mirror or tracing paper to help you. The letters for the first two shapes have been written for you.

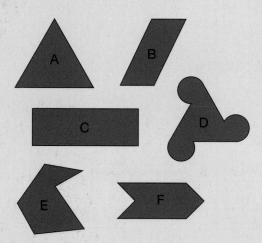

	Number of lines of symmetry			
Order of rotational symmetry	**0**	**1**	**2**	**3**
1				
2	B			
3				A

CHAPTER 15

Handling Data 3

This chapter is going to show you

- how to draw a pie chart where the data is given as percentages
- how to compare distributions using range and mean

What you should already know

- How to draw pie charts
- How to calculate the mean of a set of data
- How to find the range of a set of data

Pie charts

Sometimes information is given as a table of percentages. To draw pie charts using such data, you need to use a pie-chart scale, which is marked in hundredths rather than degrees, or a pie with ten sectors or divisions, like the one shown below.

Example 15.1 ▶

The table shows the favourite drink of 30 students in Year 7. Draw a pie chart to show the data.

Milk	9
Coke	12
Coffee	6
Tea	3

The data adds up to 30 people, so each division on the pie chart represents 3 people.

This means that Milk gets 3 divisions (as 3 × 3 = 9), Coke gets 4 divisions, and so on.

Make sure the chart is labelled.

Example 15.2 ▶

The two tables below show the lateness of trains in Britain and Spain. Draw pie charts to show both sets of data. Write a sentence to compare the punctuality of trains in both countries.

Lateness: Britain	Percentage
On time	55
Up to 5 minutes late	10
Between 5 and 10 minutes late	15
More than 10 minutes late	20

Lateness: Spain	Percentage
On time	85
Up to 5 minutes late	10
Between 5 and 10 minutes late	5
More than 10 minutes late	0

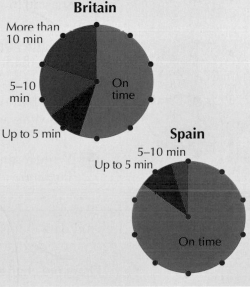

Each division on the pie represents 10%.

More trains in Britain are over 5 minutes late.

For each of the pie charts, start with a copy of the circle that is divided into ten sectors. Remember to label your pie chart.

1 Draw a pie chart to show the data in each table.

a Colours of 20 cars in a car park.

Colour	No. of cars
Red	4
Blue	7
Green	3
Yellow	2
Black	4

b Pets of 30 Year 7 students.

Pet	No. of pets
Dog	9
Cat	6
Bird	3
Fish	3
Gerbil	9

c Favourite subjects of 100 Year 11 students.

Subject	% of students
Maths	45
English	15
Geography	20
History	10
Games	10

d Favourite soap operas of 100 Year 7 students.

Soap opera	% of students
Eastenders	60
Coronation St	20
Emmerdale	10
Brookside	10

e Percentage distribution of age groups in Rotherham.

Age	% of population
Under 16	15
16–25	20
26–40	30
41–60	20
Over 60	15

f Percentage distribution of age groups in Eastbourne.

Age	% of population
Under 16	10
16–25	15
26–40	25
41–60	20
Over 60	30

2 Write a sentence about the difference in the age distributions between Rotherham, which is an industrial city in the north of England, and Eastbourne, which is a seaside town on the south coast.

3 Is it true, or maybe you cannot say, that there are more people under 16 in Rotherham than in Eastbourne? Give a reason for your answer.

4 The chart on the left is the distribution of ages in an Indian village. Draw a table to show the age distribution, like the tables in Question 1.

5 Write a sentence about the differences between the age distribution in India and in England.

Extension Work

Find data that is given as percentages. For example, the table of constituents on the side of a cereal packet.

Draw pie charts to compare these and display them as a poster.

Comparing data

Example 15.3

You are organising a ten-pin bowling match. You have one team place to fill.

These are the last five scores for Carol and Doris.

Carol	122	131	114	162	146
Doris	210	91	135	99	151

Who would you pick to be in the team and why?

The mean for Carol is 135 and the range is 48.
The mean for Doris is 137.2 and the range is 119.

You could pick Doris as she has the greater mean, or you could pick Carol as she is more consistent.

Example 15.4

Your teacher thinks that the girls in the class are absent more often than the boys.

There are 10 boys in your class. Their days absent over last term were:

5   0   3   4   6   3   0   8   6   5

There are 12 girls in the class. Their days absent over last term were:

2   1   0   0   5   3   1   2   3   50   2   3

Is your teacher correct? Explain your answer.

The mean for the boys is 4 and the range is 8.
The mean for the girls is 6 and the range is 50.

It looks as though your teacher is correct. But if you take out the girl who was absent 50 times because she was in hospital, the mean for the girls becomes 2 and the range 5. In that case, your teacher would be wrong.

Exercise 15B

1 You have to choose someone to play darts for your team. You ask Bill and Ben to throw ten times each. These are their scores.

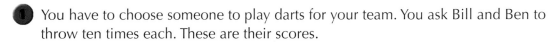

Bill	32	16	25	65	12	24	63	121	31	11
Ben	43	56	40	31	37	49	49	30	31	24

a Work out the mean for Bill. **b** Work out the range for Bill.

c Work out the mean for Ben. **d** Work out the range for Ben.

e Who would you choose and why?

2 You have to catch a bus regularly. You can catch bus A or bus B. On the last ten times you caught these buses. You noted down, in minutes, how late they were.

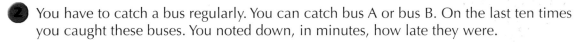

Bus A	1	2	4	12	1	3	5	6	2	9
Bus B	6	5	5	6	2	4	4	5	6	7

a Work out the mean for bus A. **b** Work out the range for bus A.

c Work out the mean for bus B. **d** Work out the range for bus B.

e Which bus would you catch and why?

Write your own statistical report on one or more of the following problems.
For these problems, you will need to use secondary sources to collect the data.

1   Do football teams in the First Division score more goals than teams in
    the Second Division?

2   Compare the frequency of letters in the English language to the frequency
    of letters in the French language.

3   Compare the prices of second-hand cars using different motoring
    magazines.

Comparing experimental and theoretical probabilities

This section will remind you how to calculate the probabilities of events where the
outcomes are equally likely. You will also see how to compare your calculations with
what happens in practice by carrying out experiments to find the experimental
probabilities of these events.

The **theoretical probability** of an event predicts what is likely to happen when you know
all the possible outcomes of the event. You can use theoretical probability only when all
the outcomes are equally likely.

For theoretical probability:

$$P(\text{event}) = \frac{\text{Number of ways the event can happen}}{\text{Total number of all possible outcomes}}$$

Finding the **experimental probability** of an event lets you check the theoretical
probability and see whether an experiment is fair or unfair. To calculate the experimental
probability, you carry out a sequence of repeated experiments or **trials**.

For experimental probability:

$$P(\text{event}) = \frac{\text{Number of events in the trials}}{\text{Total number of trials}}$$

Remember: the more trials you carry out, the closer the experimental probability gets to
the theoretical probability.

Example 15.5 ▷

Josie wants to compare the experimental probability for the event Heads happening
when she tosses a coin with the theoretical probability to see whether the coin she is
using is a fair one.

Josie decides to carry out 50 trials and completes the frequency table given below.

	Tally					Frequency
Heads	ℍℍℍ	ℍℍℍ	ℍℍℍ	ℍℍℍ	ℍℍℍ II	27
Tails	ℍℍℍ	ℍℍℍ	ℍℍℍ	ℍℍℍ III		23

Example 15.5
continued

The experimental probability for the event Heads is

$$P(\text{Heads}) = \frac{27}{50}$$

Josie knows that there are two equally likely outcomes, Heads or Tails, when she tosses a coin. So, the theoretical trial probability is given by:

$$P(\text{Heads}) = \frac{1}{2}$$

She can now compare the two probabilities. To do this, she needs to change each probability fraction into a decimal to make the comparison easier.

$$\frac{27}{50} = 0.54 \text{ and } \frac{1}{2} = 0.5$$

The two decimals are close. So she concludes that the coin is a fair one.

Exercise 15D

1 a Working in pairs, throw a four-sided dice 40 times and record your results on a copy of the following frequency table.

Score	Tally	Frequency
1		
2		
3		
4		

Use your results to find the experimental probability of getting
  i 4   **ii** an even number

b Write down the theoretical probability of getting
  i 4   **ii** an even number

c By writing your answers to parts **a** and **b** as decimals, state whether you think the dice is a fair one or not.

2 Put ten cards numbered 1 to 10 in a box. Working in pairs, pick a card from the box and note its number. Replace it, shake the box and pick another card. Repeat the experiment 20 times and record your results in a frequency table.

a Use your results to find the experimental probability of getting
  i 10   **ii** an odd number

b Write down the theoretical probability of getting
  i 10   **ii** an odd number

c Compare your answers to parts **a** and **b**, and state any conclusions you make about the experiment.

3 You will need a box or a bag containing two red counters, three green counters and five blue counters.

a Working in pairs, pick a counter from the box and note its colour. Replace it, shake the box and pick another counter. Repeat the experiment 50 times and record your results on a copy of the following frequency table.

Colour	Tally	Frequency
Red		
Green		
Blue		

Use your results to find the experimental probability of getting

   i a red counter   **ii** a green counter   **iii** a blue counter

b Write down the theoretical probability of getting

   i a red counter   **ii** a green counter   **iii** a blue counter

c By writing your answers to parts **a** and **b** as decimals, state whether you think the experiment is fair or not.

Extension Work

For this activity, you will need to work in pairs or groups.

On a large sheet of paper or card, draw a square measuring 40 cm by 40 cm. Divide into 100 squares, each measuring 4 cm by 4 cm.

- Each person rolls a 2p coin onto the sheet 50 times.
- If the coin lands completely inside a small square, score 1 point.
- If the coin touches or covers any line when it lands, score 0 point.
- The winner is the person who gets the most points.
- Work out the experimental probability of coin landing completely inside a small square.
- You often see games like this one at fun fairs and village fêtes. Do you think these games are fair?

What you need to know for level 4

- How to collect data and record it in a frequency table
- Understand and be able to use the range to describe a set of data

What you need to know for level 5

- How to compare two distributions using the mean and the range, and to draw conclusions
- How to construct and interpret pie charts
- How to calculate probabilities based on experimental evidence

LEVEL 4

1 *1997 Paper 2*

There are 50 children altogether in a playgroup.

a How many of the children are girls?
What percentage of the children are girls?

b 25 of the children are 4 years old.
20 of the children are 3 years old.
5 of the children are 2 years old.

Show this information on a copy of the
diagram on the right.

Label each part clearly.

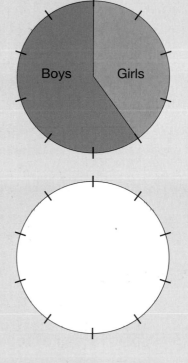

LEVEL 5

2 *1993 Paper 2*

Rita and Yoko counted the numbers of chips they got from two school dinner servers. This is
what they found out:

	Number of chips									
Server 1	32	33	34	35	33	31	34	33	35	30
Server 2	39	26	25	26	39	27	40	39	39	40

They worked out the mean for each server.

They decided server 2 was better
because the mean was bigger.

	Mean
Server 1	33
Server 2	34

Then they worked out the range for each server.

Say why the low range for server 1 was good.

	Range
Server 1	5
Server 2	15

3 *1998 Paper 2*

These pie charts show some information about the ages of people in Greece and in Ireland.

There are about 10 million people in Greece, and there are about 3.5 million people in Ireland.

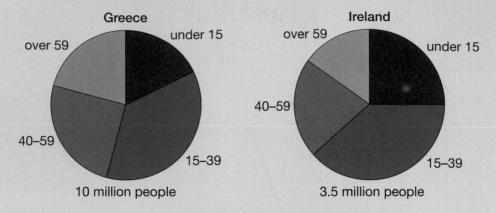

10 million people   3.5 million people

a Roughly what percentage of people in Greece are aged 40–59?

b There are about 10 million people in Greece. Use your percentage from part **a** to work out roughly how many people in Greece are aged 40–59.

c Dewi says:

The charts show that there are more people under 15 in Ireland than in Greece.

Dewi is wrong. Explain why the charts do not show this.

d There are about 60 million people in the UK. The table shows roughly what percentage of people in the UK are of different ages.

Under 15	15–39	40–59	Over 59
20%	35%	25%	20%

Draw on a copy of the pie chart (next to the table) the information in the table. Label each section of your pie chart clearly with the ages.

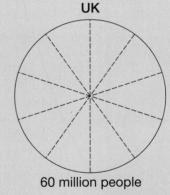

UK

60 million people

4 *2000 Paper 2*

A school has a new canteen. A special person will be chosen to perform the opening ceremony.

The names of all the pupils, all the teachers and all the canteen staff are put into a box. One name is taken out at random.

A pupil says:

'There are only three choices. It could be a pupil, a teacher or one of the canteen staff. The probabiliy of it being a pupil is $\frac{1}{3}$.'

The pupil is wrong. Explain why.

This chapter is going to show you

- how to multiply and divide decimals by whole numbers
- how to use the memory keys on a calculator
- how to use the square root and sign change keys on a calculator
- how to calculate fractions and percentages of quantities

What you should already know

- How to do long and short multiplication and division
- Equivalence of fractions, decimals and percentages
- How to use a calculator efficiently, including the use of brackets

Adding and subtracting decimals

You have already met addition and subtraction of decimals in Chapter 2. In this section, you will be doing problems involving whole numbers, decimals and metric units.

Example 16.1

Work out **a** $4 + 0.86 + 0.07$ **b** $6 - 1.45$

a   Whole numbers have a decimal point after the units digit. So, put in zeros for the missing place values, and line up the decimal points:

$$
\begin{array}{r}
4.00 \\
0.86 \\
+\ 0.07 \\
\hline
4.93 \\
{\scriptstyle 1}
\end{array}
$$

b   As in the previous sum, put in zeros to make up the missing place values, and line up the decimal points:

$$
\begin{array}{r}
{\scriptstyle 5\ \ 9\ 1} \\
6.00 \\
-\ 1.45 \\
\hline
4.55
\end{array}
$$

Example 16.2

Nazia has done 4.3 km of a 20 km bike ride. How far does Nazia still have to go?

The units are the same, so

$$
\begin{array}{r}
{\scriptstyle 1\ 9\ 1} \\
20.0 \\
-\ \ \ 4.3 \\
\hline
15.7
\end{array}
$$

Nazia still has to go 15.7 km.

Example 16.3 ▶

Mary wants to lose 3 kg in weight. So far she has lost 650 grams. How much more does she need to lose?

The units need to made the same. So change 650 grams into 0.65 kg. This gives:

$$\begin{array}{r} {}^{2}\cancel{3}{}^{9}.{}^{1}00 \\ -\ 0.65 \\ \hline 2.35 \end{array}$$

Mary still has to lose 2.35 kg.

Exercise 16A

1 Without using a calculator, work out each of these.

a $3.2 + 1.28$ b $2.56 + 1.39$ c $2.74 + 1.45$ d $2.47 + 1.28$

e $52.12 + 23.23 + 0.94 + 1.72$ f $23.54 + 36.29 + 0.24 + 6.3$

g $31.73 + 42.96 + 23.72 + 1.83$ h $32.43 + 12 + 22.82 + 106.6$

i $5 + 203.07 + 0.56$ j $0.08 + 6 + 7.1 + 9.94$

2 Without using a calculator, work out each of these.

a $4 - 2.38$ b $5 - 1.29$ c $8 - 3.14$ d $12 - 2.38$

e $7 - 1.08$ f $10 - 2.66$ g $24 - 12.3$ h $15 - 6.09$

3 The diagram shows the lengths of the paths in a park.

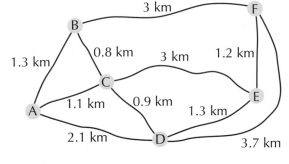

a How long are the paths altogether?

b John wants to visit all the points A, B, C, D, E and F in this order. He wants to start and finish at A and go along each and every path. Explain why he cannot do this in the distance you worked out for part **a**.

c Work out the shortest distance John could walk if he wanted to visit each point, starting and finishing at A.

4 A Christmas cake weighs 2 kg. Arthur takes a slice weighing 235 grams. How much is left?

5 23 cl of water is poured from a jug containing 3 litres. How much is left?

6 1560 millimetres of ribbon is cut from a roll that is 5 metres long. How much ribbon is left?

7 The three legs of a relay are 3 km, 4.8 km and 1800 m. How far is the race altogether?

8 Three packages weigh 4 kg, 750 grams and 0.08 kg. How much do they weigh altogether?

Write down all the pairs of single-digit numbers that add up to 9: for example, 2 + 7.

By looking at your answers to Question 2 in Exercise 16A and working out the following

a   1 − 0.435   **b**   6 − 2.561   **c**   12 − 3.6754

explain how you can just write down the answers when you are taking away a decimal from a whole number.

Make a poster to explain this to a Year 6 student.

Multiplying and dividing decimals

When you add together 1.2 + 1.2 + 1.2 + 1.2, you get 4.8.

This sum can be written as 4 × 1.2 = 4.8. It can also be written as 4.8 ÷ 4 = 1.2.

You are now going to look at how to multiply and divide decimals by whole numbers.

These two operations are just like any type of division and multiplication but you need to be sure where to put the decimal point. As a general rule, there will be the same number of decimal places in the answer as there were in the original problem.

Example 16.4 Work out **a**   5 × 3.7   **b**   8 × 4.3   **c**   9 × 1.08   **d**   6 × 3.5

Each of these can be set out in a column:

a   3.7
   $\times$ 5
   ─────
   18.5
     ₃

b   4.3
   $\times$ 8
   ─────
   34.4
     ₂

c   1.08
   $\times$ 9
   ─────
   9.72
     ₇

d   3.5
   $\times$ 6
   ─────
   21.0
     ₃

You see that the decimal point stays in the *same* place. You would give the answer to part **d** as 21.

Example 16.5 Work out **a**   22.8 ÷ 6   **b**   33.6 ÷ 7   **c**   9.59 ÷ 7   **d**   26.2 ÷ 5

These can be set out as short division:

a   3.8
      6)22.⁴8

b   4.8
      7)33.⁵6

c   1.37
      7)9.²5⁴9

d   5.24
      5)26.¹2⁰0

Once again, the decimal point stays in the same place. Notice that a zero had to be put in part **d**.

Exercise 16B

1 Without using a calculator, work out each of these.

   a   3.14 × 5   **b**   1.73 × 8   **c**   1.41 × 6   **d**   2.26 × 9
   e   6 × 3.35   **f**   9 × 5.67   **g**   5 × 6.17   **h**   9 × 9.12

2 Without using a calculator, work out each of these.

   a   17.04 ÷ 8   **b**   39.2 ÷ 7   **c**   27.2 ÷ 8   **d**   30.6 ÷ 5
   e   25.88 ÷ 4   **f**   4.44 ÷ 3   **g**   27.72 ÷ 9   **h**   22.4 ÷ 5

3 A piece of wood, 2.8 metres long, is cut into five equal pieces. How long is each piece?

4 Five bars of metal each weigh 2.35 kg. How much do they weigh together?

5 A cake weighing 1.74 kg is cut into six equal pieces. How much does each piece weigh?

6 Eight bottles of pop cost £6.24. How much is one bottle?

7 One floppy disk holds 1.44 Mb of information. How much information will six floppy disks hold?

Extension Work

Use a calculator to work out each of the following.

a 46×34 **b** 4.6×34 **c** 4.6×3.4 **d** 0.46×0.34

Try some examples of your own.

You will notice that the digits of all the answers are the same but that the decimal point is in different places. Can you see the rule for placing the decimal point?

Using a calculator

Your calculator is broken. Only the keys shown are working. Using just these keys, can you make all the numbers up to 25? For example:

    $1 = 4 - 3$ $12 = 3 \times 4$ $15 = 4 + 4 + 7$

You have already met brackets on a calculator in Chapter 9 (page 100). With the most recent calculators, using brackets is probably the best way to do lengthy calculations. The problem with keying in a calculation using brackets is that there is no intermediate working to check where you made mistakes. One way round this is to use the memory keys, or to write down the intermediate values. (This is what examiners call 'working'.)

The memory is a location inside the calculator where a number can be stored.

The memory keys are not exactly the same on different makes of calculators, but they all do the same things. Let's look at the four main keys:

Min   This key puts the value in the display into the memory and the contents of the memory are lost. This is STO on some calculators.

M+   This key adds the contents of the display to the contents of the memory.

M–   This key subtracts the contents of the display from the contents of the memory. This is SHIFT M+ on some calculators.

MR   This key recalls the contents of the memory and puts it in the display. The contents of the display will disappear but may still be involved in the calculation.

Example 16.6 ▷

Calculate **a** $\dfrac{16.8 + 28.8}{23.8 - 16.2}$ **b** $60.3 \div (16.3 - 9.6)$

a Type in 23.8 – 16.2 =, which gives an answer of 7.6. Store this in the memory with Min.

Type in 16.8 + 28.8 =, which gives 45.6 in the display. Type ÷ MR =. This should give an answer of 6.

b Type in 16.3 – 9.6 =, which gives an answer of 6.7. Store this with Min.

Type in 60.3 ÷ MR =, which should give an answer of 9.

Two other very useful keys are the square root key $\boxed{\sqrt{}}$ and the sign change key $\boxed{+/_-}$.

Note that not all calculators have a sign change key. Some have $\boxed{(-)}$. Also, the square root key has to be pressed before the number on some calculators and after the number on others.

The best thing to do is to get your own calculator and learn how to use it.

Example 16.7 ▷

Calculate **a** $\sqrt{432}$ **b** $180 - (32 + 65)$

a Either √ 432 = or 432 √ = should give 20.78460969. Round this off to 20.78.

b Type in 32 + 65 =, which should give 97. Press the sign change key and the display should change to –97. Type in +180 =, which should give 83.

The sign change key is also used to input a negative number. For example, on some calculators, 2 $\boxed{+/_-}$ will give a display of –2.

Exercise 16C

1 Use the memory keys to work out each of the following. Write down any values that you store in the memory.

    a $\dfrac{17.8 + 25.6}{14.5 - 8.3}$ **b** $\dfrac{35.7 - 19.2}{34.9 - 19.9}$ **c** $\dfrac{16.9 + 23.6}{16.8 - 14.1}$ **d** $\dfrac{47.2 - 19.6}{11.1 - 8.8}$

    e $45.6 - (23.4 - 6.9)$ **f** $44.8 \div (12.8 - 7.2)$ **g** $(4 \times 28.8) \div (9.5 - 3.1)$

2 Use the sign change key to enter the first negative number. Then use the calculator to work out the value of each of these.

    a $-2 + 3 - 7$ **b** $-4 - 6 + 8$ **c** $-6 + 7 - 8 + 2$ **d** $-5 + 3 - 8 + 9$

3 Use the square root key to work out

    a $\sqrt{400}$ **b** $\sqrt{300}$ **c** $\sqrt{150}$ **d** $\sqrt{10}$

4 What happens if you press the sign key twice in succession?

5 If you start with 16 and press the square root key twice in succession, the display shows 2. If you start with 81 and press the square root key twice in succession, the display shows 3.

Explain what numbers are shown in the display.

6 Calculate each of the following **i** using the brackets keys, and **ii** using the memory keys.

Write out the key presses for each. Which method uses fewer key presses?

a $\dfrac{12.9 + 42.9}{23.7 - 14.4}$ **b** $\dfrac{72.4 - 30.8}{16.85 - 13.6}$ **c** $25.6 \div (6.7 - 3.5)$

Extension Work

It helps to understand how a calculator works if you can think like a calculator. So, do the following without using a calculator.

You are told what the number in the memory and the number in the display are.

After each series of operations shown below, what number will be in the display and what number will be in the memory? The first one has been done as an example.

	Starting number in display	Starting number in memory	Operations	Final number in display	Final number in memory
	6	10	M+, M+, M+	6	28
a	6	10	Min, M+, M+		
b	6	10	M−, MR		
c	12	5	M+, MR, M+		
d	10	6	M+, M+, M+, MR		
e	10	6	MR, M+, M+		
f	8	8	M−, M+, MR, M+		
g	15	20	M−, M−, MR, M+		

Fractions of quantities

This section is going to help you to revise the rules for working with fractions.

Example 16.8 Find **a** $\frac{2}{7}$ of £28 **b** $\frac{3}{5}$ of 45 sweets **c** $1\frac{2}{3}$ of 15 m

a First, find $\frac{1}{7}$ of £28: $28 \div 7 = 4$. So, $\frac{2}{7}$ of £28 = $2 \times 4 = £8$.

b First, find $\frac{1}{5}$ of 45 sweets: $45 \div 5 = 9$. So, $\frac{3}{5}$ of 45 sweets = $3 \times 9 = 27$ sweets.

c Either calculate $\frac{2}{3}$ of 15 and add it to 15, or make $1\frac{2}{3}$ into a top-heavy fraction and work out $\frac{5}{3}$ of 15.

$15 \div 3 = 5$, so $\frac{2}{3}$ of 15 = 10. Hence, $1\frac{2}{3}$ of 15 m = 15 + 10 = 25 m.

$15 \div 3 = 5$, so $\frac{5}{3}$ of 15 = 25 m.

Example 16.9 ▷ Find **a** $7 \times \frac{3}{4}$ **b** $8 \times \frac{2}{3}$ **c** $5 \times 1\frac{3}{5}$

a $7 \times \frac{3}{4} = \frac{21}{4} = 5\frac{1}{4}$.

b $8 \times \frac{2}{3} = \frac{16}{3} = 5\frac{1}{3}$.

c $5 \times 1\frac{3}{5} = 5 \times \frac{8}{5} = \frac{40}{5} = 8$.

Example 16.10 ▷ A magazine has 96 pages. $\frac{5}{12}$ of the pages have adverts on them. How many pages have adverts on them?

$\frac{1}{12}$ of 96 = 8. So, $\frac{5}{12}$ of 96 = 5 × 8 = 40 pages.

Exercise 16D

1 Find each of these.

a $\frac{2}{3}$ of £27 **b** $\frac{3}{5}$ of 75 kg **c** $1\frac{2}{3}$ of 18 metres **d** $\frac{4}{9}$ of £18

e $\frac{3}{10}$ of £46 **f** $\frac{5}{8}$ of 840 houses **g** $\frac{3}{7}$ of 21 litres **h** $1\frac{2}{5}$ of 45 minutes

i $\frac{5}{6}$ of £63 **j** $\frac{3}{8}$ of 1600 loaves **k** $1\frac{4}{7}$ of 35 km **l** $\frac{7}{10}$ of 600 crows

m $\frac{2}{9}$ of £1.26 **n** $\frac{4}{9}$ of 540 children **o** $\frac{7}{12}$ of 144 miles **p** $3\frac{3}{11}$ of £22.

2 Find each of these as a mixed number.

a $5 \times \frac{3}{4}$ **b** $8 \times \frac{2}{7}$ **c** $6 \times 1\frac{2}{3}$ **d** $4 \times \frac{3}{8}$

e $9 \times \frac{1}{4}$ **f** $5 \times 1\frac{5}{6}$ **g** $9 \times \frac{4}{5}$ **h** $7 \times 2\frac{3}{4}$

i $3 \times 3\frac{3}{7}$ **j** $8 \times \frac{2}{11}$ **k** $4 \times 1\frac{2}{7}$ **l** $6 \times \frac{7}{9}$

m $2 \times 3\frac{3}{4}$ **n** $3 \times \frac{7}{10}$ **o** $5 \times 1\frac{3}{10}$ **p** $2 \times 10\frac{5}{8}$

3 A bag of rice weighed 1300 g. $\frac{2}{5}$ of it was used to make a meal. How much was left?

4 Mrs Smith weighed 96 kg. She lost $\frac{3}{8}$ of her weight due to a diet. How much did she weigh after the diet?

5 A petrol tank holds 52 litres. $\frac{3}{4}$ is used on a journey. How many litres are left?

6 A GCSE textbook has 448 pages. $\frac{3}{28}$ of the pages are the answers. How many pages of answers are there?

7 A bar of chocolate weighs $\frac{5}{8}$ of a kilogram. How much do seven bars weigh?

8 A Smartie machine produces 1400 Smarties a minute. $\frac{2}{7}$ of them are red. How many red Smarties will the machine produce in an hour?

9 A farmer has nine cows. Each cow eats $1\frac{2}{3}$ bales of silage a week. How much do they eat altogether?

10 A cake recipe requires $\frac{2}{3}$ of a cup of walnuts. How many cups of walnuts will be needed for five cakes?

This is about dividing fractions by a whole number.

Dividing a fraction by 2 has the same effect as halving the fraction. For example:

$$\tfrac{2}{7} \div 2 = \tfrac{2}{7} \times \tfrac{1}{2} = \tfrac{1}{7}$$

Work out each of the following.

a $\tfrac{2}{3} \div 2$ **b** $\tfrac{3}{4} \div 2$ **c** $\tfrac{4}{5} \div 2$ **d** $\tfrac{7}{8} \div 2$

e $\tfrac{4}{7} \div 3$ **f** $\tfrac{2}{5} \div 5$ **g** $\tfrac{3}{8} \div 4$ **h** $\tfrac{3}{10} \div 5$

Percentages of quantities

This section will help you to revise the equivalence between fractions, percentages and decimals. It will also show you how to calculate simple percentages of quantities.

Example 16.11

Write down the equivalent percentage and fraction for each of these decimals.

a 0.6 **b** 0.28

To change a decimal to a percentage, multiply by 100. This gives: **a** 60% **b** 28%

To change a decimal to a fraction, multiply and divide by 10, 100, 1000 as appropriate and cancel if possible. This gives:

a $0.6 = \dfrac{6}{10} = \dfrac{3}{5}$ **b** $0.28 = \dfrac{28}{100} = \dfrac{7}{25}$

Example 16.12

Write down the equivalent percentage and decimal for each of these fractions.

a $\dfrac{7}{20}$ **b** $\dfrac{9}{25}$

To change a fraction into a percentage, make the denominator 100. This gives:

a $\dfrac{7}{20} = \dfrac{35}{100} = 35\%$ **b** $\dfrac{9}{25} = \dfrac{36}{100} = 36\%$

To change a fraction into a decimal, divide the top by the bottom, or make into a percentage, then divide by 100. This gives:

a 0.35 **b** 0.36

Example 16.13

Write down the equivalent decimal and fraction for each of these percentages.

a 95% **b** 26%

To convert a percentage to a decimal, divide by 100. This gives: **a** 0.95 **b** 0.26

To convert a percentage to a fraction, make a fraction over 100 then cancel if possible. This gives:

a $95\% = \dfrac{95}{100} = \dfrac{19}{20}$ **b** $26\% = \dfrac{26}{100} = \dfrac{13}{50}$

Example 16.14

Calculate   **a**   15% of £670   **b**   40% of £34

Calculate 10%, then use multiples of this.

a   10% of £670 = £67, 5% = 33.50. So, 15% of £670 = 67 + 33.5 = £100.50.

b   10% of £34 = £3.40. So, 40% of £34 = 4 × 3.40 = £13.60.

Exercise 16E

1 Copy and complete this table.

	a	b	c	d	e	f	g	h	i	j
Decimal	0.45			0.76			0.36			0.85
Fraction	$\frac{9}{20}$	$\frac{3}{5}$			$\frac{4}{25}$			$\frac{3}{50}$		
Percentage	45%		32%			37.5%			65%	

2 Calculate

   a   35% of £340   **b**   15% of £250   **c**   60% of £18   **d**   20% of £14.40

   e   45% of £440   **f**   5% of £45   **g**   40% of £5.60   **h**   25% of £24.40

3 A Jumbo Jet carries 400 passengers. On one trip, 52% of the passengers were British, 17% were American, 12% were French and the rest were German.

   a   How many people of each nationality were on the plane?

   b   What percentage were German?

4 Copy the cross-number puzzle. Use the clues to fill it in. Then use the puzzle to fill in the missing numbers in the clues.

Across

1   71% of 300
3   73% of 200
5   107% of 200
8   58% of ......
9   88% of 400

Down

1   96% of ......
2   81% of ......
3   50% of 24
4   25% of 596
6   61% of 200
7   100% of 63

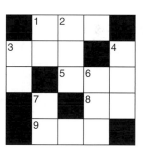

Extension Work

Copy the cross-number puzzle. Work out each percentage.
Then use the puzzle to fill in the missing numbers in the clues.

Across

1   54 out of 200
3   33 out of 50
5   13 out of 25
8   99 out of 100
10   ...... out of 200
12   27 out of 50
14   38 out of 200

Down

2   ...... out of 400
4   134 out of 200
6   ...... out of 300
7   100 out of 400
9   ...... out of 20
11   110 out of 1000
13   23 out of 50

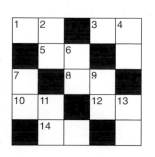

Solving problems

Below are two investigations. Before you start either of these, read the question carefully and think about how you are going to record your results. Show all your working clearly.

Who wants to be a millionaire?

You have won a prize in a lottery. You have a choice of how to take the prize.

You can either:

Take £10 000 in the first year, 10% less (£9000) in the second year, 10% less than the second year's amount (£8100) in the third year, and so on for 10 years.

Or

Take £1000 in the first year, 50% more (£1500) in the second year, 50% more than the second year's amount (£1500) in the third year, and so on for 10 years.

You will probably need to use a calculator and round off the amounts to the nearest penny.

What would happen if the second method gave 40% more each year?

What would happen if the second method started with £10 000?

Chocolate bars

Eight children, Alf, Betty, Charles, Des, Ethel, Fred, George and Helen, are lined up outside a room in alphabetical order.

Inside the room are three tables. Each table has eight chairs around it.

On the first table is one chocolate bar, on the second table are two chocolate bars, and on the third table are three chocolate bars.

The children go into the room one at a time and sit at one of the tables. After they are all seated they share out the chocolate bars on the table at which they are seated.

Where should Alf sit to make sure he gets the most chocolate?

What you need to know for level 4

- How to solve problems and apply mathematics to practical contexts
- How to present results in a clear and organised way
- How to use simple fractions and percentages to describe proportions of a whole

What you need to know for level 5

- How to carry through a task and solve mathematical problems, and identify and obtain the necessary information
- How to check results and describe situations using mathematical symbols, words and diagrams
- How to calculate fractions and percentages of quantities and of measurements

LEVEL 4

1 *2000 Paper 1*

Mark and James have the same birthday. They were born on 15th March in different years.

a Mark will be 12 years old on 15 March 2001.

How old will he be on 15 March 2010?

b In which year was Mark born?

c James was half of Mark's age on 15 March 2001. In what year was James born?

2 *2001 Paper 2*

Look at this number chain.

a Fill in the missing numbers in the circles below.

b Fill in the missing numbers in the arrows below.

LEVEL 5

3 *1998 Paper 2*

You can make different colours of paint by mixing red, blue and yellow in different proportions. For example, you can make green by mixing one part blue to one part yellow.

a To make purple, you mix 3 parts red to 7 parts blue.
How much of each colour do you need to make 20 litres of purple paint?

b To make orange, you mix 13 parts yellow to 7 parts red.
How much of each colour do you need to make 10 litres of orange paint?

4 *1998 Paper 1*

a A teacher needs 220 booklets. The booklets are in packs of 16.
How many packs must the teacher order?

b Each booklet weighs 48 g. How much do the 220 booklets weigh altogether? Give your answer in kg.

This chapter is going to show you

o how to use the algebraic ideas given in previous chapters
o how to extend these ideas into more difficult problems

What you should already know

o How to solve simple equations
o How to use simple formulae and derive a formula
o How to find the term-to-term rule in a sequence
o How to plot coordinates and draw graphs
o How to use algebra to solve simple problems

Solving equations

In Chapter 6 (page 72) you were shown how to solve the types of equation in Examples 17.1 and 17.2.

Example 17.1 ▶

Solve $5x + 12 = 87$.

Subtract 12 from both sides:
$$5x + 12 - 12 = 87 - 12$$
$$5x = 75$$

Divide both sides by 5:
$$\frac{5x}{5} = \frac{75}{5}$$
$$x = 15$$

Example 17.2 ▶

Solve $13x - 7 = 149$.

Add 7 to both sides:
$$13x - 7 + 7 = 149 + 7$$
$$13x = 156$$

Divide both sides by 13:
$$\frac{13x}{13} = \frac{156}{13}$$
$$x = 12$$

Exercise 17A

● Solve each of the following equations.

a $11x = 121$	**b** $13x = 117$	**c** $15x = 195$	**d** $14x = 98$
e $13m = 182$	**f** $15m = 120$	**g** $17m = 323$	**h** $14m = 70$
i $16k = 336$	**j** $15k = 90$	**k** $13k = 221$	**l** $12k = 36$
m $17x = 578$	**n** $42x = 504$	**p** $53x = 371$	**q** $91x = 1456$

● Solve each of the following equations.

   a $x + 23 = 35$ **b** $x + 13 = 21$ **c** $x + 18 = 30$ **d** $x + 48 = 54$

   e $m + 44 = 57$ **f** $m - 13 = 4$ **g** $k - 12 = 6$ **h** $p - 15 = -9$

   i $k + 72 = 95$ **j** $k - 12 = -5$ **k** $m + 33 = 49$ **l** $x - 13 = -8$

   m $x + 85 = 112$ **n** $n - 21 = -10$ **p** $m - 15 = -9$ **q** $x + 12 = 37$

● Solve the following equations.

   a $12x + 3 = 51$ **b** $21x + 5 = 257$ **c** $13x + 4 = 108$

   d $32x + 7 = 359$ **e** $14m + 1 = 253$ **f** $15k + 6 = 81$

   g $4n + 9 = 65$ **h** $12x + 7 = 199$ **i** $6h + 5 = 119$

   j $7t + 5 = 68$ **k** $8x + 3 = 107$ **l** $5y + 3 = 33$

   m $17x + 3 = 292$ **n** $42t + 7 = 427$ **p** $23x + 8 = 353$

   q $8m + 3 = 51$

● Solve the following equations

   a $12x + 3 = 87$ **b** $13x + 4 = 56$ **c** $15x - 1 = 194$

   d $14x - 3 = 137$ **e** $13m - 2 = 24$ **f** $15m + 4 = 184$

   g $17m + 3 = 105$ **h** $14m - 5 = 219$ **i** $16k + 1 = 129$

   j $15k - 3 = 162$ **k** $13k - 1 = 38$ **l** $12k + 5 = 173$

   m $17x - 4 = 285$ **n** $14x + 3 = 73$ **p** $15x + 6 = 231$

   q $19x - 4 = 167$

Extension Work

1   The sum of ten consecutive numbers is the same as the number of days in a non leap year. What is the smallest of the numbers?

2   I multiply a number by 8, subtract 14 and obtain the number of weeks in a year. What is my number?

3   Make up some similar problems using numbers in times or dates.

Formulae

Formulae occur in many situations, some of which you have already met. You need to be able to use formulae to calculate a variety of quantities.

Example 17.3

One rule to find the area of a triangle is to take half of the length of its base and multiply it by the vertical height of the triangle. This rule, written as a formula is

$$A = \tfrac{1}{2}bh$$

where A = area, b = base length, and h = vertical height.

Using this formula to calculate the area of a triangle with a base length of 7 cm and a vertical height of 16 cm gives

$$\text{Area} = \tfrac{1}{2} \times 7 \times 16 = 56 \text{ cm}^2$$

1 The average of three numbers is given by the formula

$$A = \frac{m + n + p}{3}$$

where A is the average and m, n and p are the numbers.

a Use the formula to find the average of 4, 8 and 15.

b What is the average of 32, 43 and 54?

2 The perimeter of a rectangle is given by the formula

$$P = 2(m + n)$$

where P is the perimeter, m is the length and n is the width.

a Use the formula to find the perimeter of a rectangle 5 cm by 8 cm.

b Use the formula to find the perimeter of a rectangle 13 cm by 18 cm.

3 The average speed of a car is given by the formula

$$A = \frac{d}{t}$$

where A is the average speed in miles per hour, d is the number of miles travelled, and t is the number of hours taken for the journey.

a Find the average speed of a car which travels 220 miles in 4 hours.

b In 8 hours a car covered 360 miles. What was the average speed?

4 The speed, v m/s, of the train t seconds after passing through a station with a speed of u m/s, is given by the formula

$$v = u + 5t$$

a What is the speed 4 seconds after leaving a station with a speed of 12 m/s?

b What is the speed 10 seconds after leaving a station with a speed of 8 m/s?

5 The speed, v, of a land speed car can be calculated using the following formula

$$v = u + at$$

where v is the speed after t seconds, u is the initial speed, and a is the acceleration.

a Calculate the speed of the car with 10 m/s^2 acceleration 8 seconds after it had a speed of 12 m/s.

b Calculate the speed of a car with 5 m/s^2 acceleration 12 seconds after it had a speed of 15 m/s.

6 To change a temperature in degrees Celsius to degrees Fahrenheit, we use the formula

$$F = 32 + 1.8C$$

where F is the temperature in degrees Fahrenheit and C is the temperature in degrees Celsius.

Change each of the following temperatures to degrees Fahrenheit.

a 45 °C   **b** 40 °C   **c** 65 °C   **d** 100 °C

1   When a stone is dropped from the top of a cliff, the distance, d metres, that it falls in t seconds is given by the formula

$$d = 4.9t^2$$

Calculate the distance a stone has fallen 8 seconds after being dropped from the top of a cliff.

2   The distance, D km, which you can see out to sea from the shore line, at a height of h metres above sea level, is given by the formula

$$D = \sqrt{(12.5h)}$$

How far out to sea can you see from the top of a cliff, 112 metres above sea level?

Dotty investigations

Exercise 17C

1   Look at the following two shapes drawn on a dotted square grid.

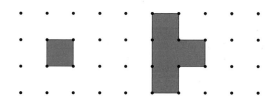

By drawing some of your own shapes (with no dots inside each shape), complete the table below, giving the number of dots on each perimeter and the area of each shape.

Number of dots on perimeter	Area of shape
4	1 cm²
6	
8	
10	4 cm²
12	
14	
16	

2   What is special about the number of dots on the perimeter of all the shapes in the table of Question 1?

● For a shape with no dots inside, one way to calculate the area of the shape from the number of dots on the perimeter is to

Divide the number of dots by two, then subtract 1

a Check that this rule works for all the shapes drawn in Question 1.

b Write this rule as a formula, where A is the area of a shape and D is the number of dots on its perimeter.

● Look at the following two shapes drawn on a dotted square grid. They both have one dot inside.

By drawing some of your own shapes (with only one dot inside each shape), complete the table below.

Number of dots on perimeter	Dots inside	Area of shape
4	1	
6	1	
8	1	4 cm²
10	1	
12	1	
14	1	
16	1	

● For the shapes in Question 4, find a formula to connect A, the area of each shape with D, the number of dots on its perimeter.

● **a** Draw some shapes with an even number of dots on each perimeter and two dots inside each shape.

b Find the formula connecting A, the area of each shape, with D, the number of dots on its perimeter.

● **a** Draw some shapes with an even number of dots on each perimeter and three dots inside each shape.

b Find the formula connecting A, the area of each shape, with D, the number of dots on its perimeter.

Graphs from the real world

When you fill your car with petrol, both the amount of petrol you've taken and its cost are displayed on the pump. One litre of petrol costs about 80p, but this rate does change from time to time.

The table below shows the costs of different quantities of petrol as displayed on a petrol pump.

Petrol (litres)	5	10	15	20	25	30
Cost (£)	4	8	12	16	20	24

This information can also be represented by the following ordered pairs:

    (5, 4)   (10, 8)   (15, 12)   (20, 16)   (25, 20)   (30, 24)

On the right is the graph which relates the cost of petrol to the quantity bought.

This is an example of a **conversion graph**. You can use it to find the cost of any quantity of petrol, or to find how much petrol can be bought for different amounts of money.

Conversion graphs are usually straight-line graphs.

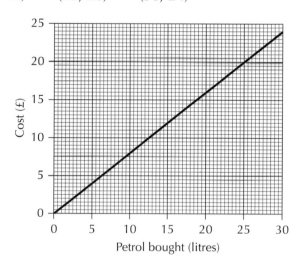

Exercise 17D

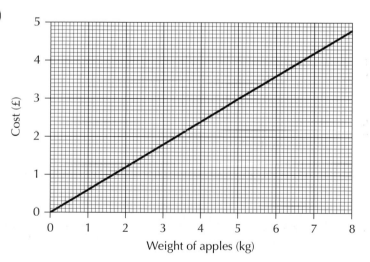

Use the graph to answer these questions
a   Find the cost of each quantity of apples.
    i   3 kg   ii   7 kg
b   What weight of apples can be bought for:
    i   £3   ii   £2.40?

2 The graph below shows the distance travelled by a car during an interval of 5 minutes.

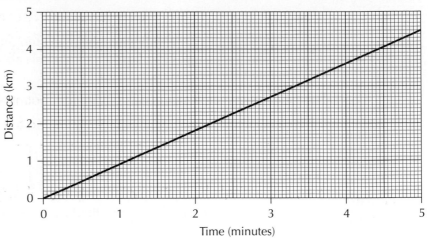

a Find the distance travelled during the second minute of the journey.

b Find the time taken to travel 3 km.

3 Here is a kilometre–mile conversion graph.

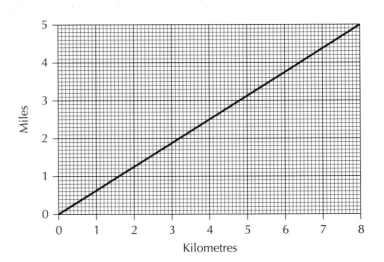

a Express each of the following distances in km:
  i 3 miles
  ii 4.5 miles

b Express each of the following distances in miles:
  i 2 km
  ii 4 km
  iii 6 km

4 a Copy and complete the following table for the exchange rate of the euro.

Euros (€)	1	5	10	15	20
Pounds (£)	0.60	3.00			

b Use the data from this table to draw a conversion graph from pounds to euros.

c Use your graph to convert each of the following to pounds.
  i €7 **ii** €16 **iii** €17.50

d Use your graph to convert each of the following to euros.
  i £9 **ii** £12 **iii** £10.80

5 A box weighs 2 kg. Packets of juice, each weighing 425 g, are packed into it.

a Draw a graph to show the weight of the box plus the packets of juice and the number of packets of fruit juice put into the box.

b Find, from the graph, the number of packets of juice that make the weight of the box and packets as close to 5 kg as possible.

A particular car could travel 6 km for every litre of diesel used by its engine. Draw a graph to show the relationship between the distance travelled (*d*) and the number of litres of diesel used (*p*). Use your graph to find each of these:

a   The distance travelled after using 12 litres of diesel.

b   The amount of diesel used by the car after travelling 90 km.

c   The equation relating the distance travelled to the amount of diesel used.

Triangle-and-circle problems

Look at the diagram on the right. The number in each box is the sum of the two numbers in the circles on each side of the box.

The values of *A*, *B* and *C* are positive integers and no two are the same. What are they?

The values of *A*, *B* and *C* can be found by using algebraic equations, as shown below.

Three equations can be written down from the diagram. They are:

$$A + B = 14 \quad (1)$$
$$B + C = 11 \quad (2)$$
$$A + C = 13 \quad (3)$$

First, add together equation (1) and equation (2). This gives

$$A + B + B + C = 14 + 11$$
$$A + 2B + C = 25 \quad (4)$$

Next, subtract equation (3) from both sides of equation (4):

$$A + 2B + C - (A + C) = 25 - 13$$
$$2B = 12$$
$$B = 6$$

Finally, substitute *B* = 6 in equations (1) and (2), to obtain *A* = 8 and *C* = 5.

1 Use algebra to solve each of these triangle-and-circle problems. All the solutions are positive integers.

a

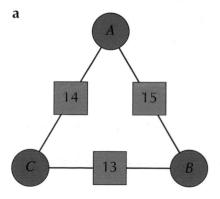

b

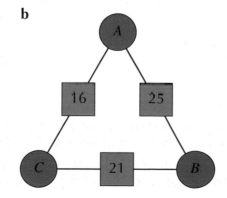

c

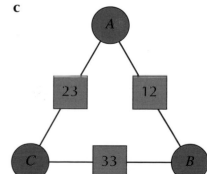

2 Use algebra to solve each of these triangle-and-circle problems. The solutions are positive and negative integers.

a

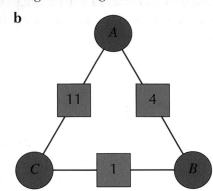

b

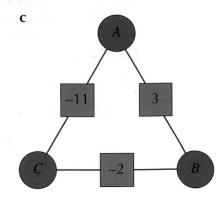

c

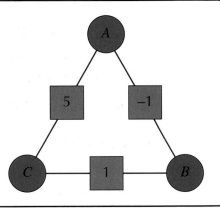

Use algebra to solve this triangle-and-circle problem.
The solutions are positive and negative numbers.

What you need to know for level 4

- How to use a simple formula expressed in words
- How to use and interpret coordinates in a simple graph
- How to solve simple equations

What you need to know for level 5

- How to construct and use simple formulae
- How to use and interpret coordinates derived from real-life situations
- How to solve equations involving two stages
- How to solve simple problems using algebra

LEVEL 4

1 *2000 Paper 2*

A book shows two ways to change °C to °F.

Exact rule	**Approximate rule**
Multiply the °C temperature by 1.8 then add 32	Double the °C temperature then add 30

a Fill in the gaps.

Using the exact rule, 25 °C is ...... °F

Using the approximate rule, 25 °C is ...... °F.

b Fill in the gaps.

Using the exact rule, 0 °C is ...... °F

Using the approximate rule, 0 °C is ...... °F

c Show that at 10 °C, the exact rule and the approximate rule give the same answers.

2 *1995 Paper 2*

Marc has ten square tiles like this:

Marc places all the square tiles in a row.
He starts his row as shown below:

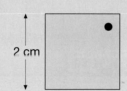

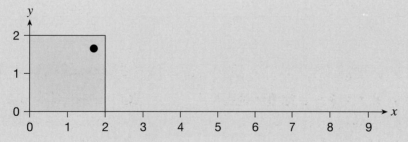

For each square tile, he writes down the coordinates of the corner which has a ●. The coordinates of the first corner are (2, 2).

a Write down the coordinates of the next five corners which have a ●.

b Look at the numbers in the coordinates. Describe two things you notice.

c Marc things that (17, 2) are the coordinates of one of the corners which have a ●. Explain why he is wrong.

d Sam has some bigger square tiles, like this:

She places them next to each other in a row, like Marc's tiles. Write down the coordinates of the first two corners which have a ◆.

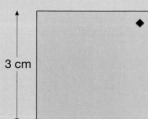

LEVEL 5

3 *1996 Paper 2*

Steve is making a series of patterns with black and grey square tiles.

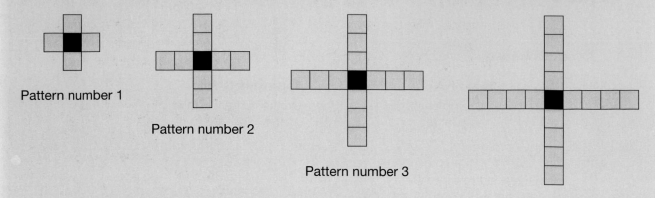

Pattern number 1

Pattern number 2

Pattern number 3

Pattern number 4

a Each pattern has one black tile at the centre.

Each new pattern has more grey tiles than the one before.

How many more grey tiles does Steve add each time he makes a new pattern?

b Steve says:

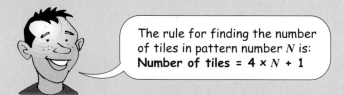

The rule for finding the number of tiles in pattern number N is:
Number of tiles = 4 × N + 1

The 1 in Steve's rule represents the black tile. What does the $4 \times N$ represent?

c Steve wants to make pattern number 15. How many black tiles and how many grey tiles does he need?

d Steve uses 41 tiles altogether to make a pattern. What is the number of the pattern he makes?

e Steve has 12 black tiles and 80 grey tiles. What is the number of the biggest pattern Steve can make?

CHAPTER 18

Shape, Space and Measures 5

<table>
<tr><td>**This chapter is going to show you**</td><td>**What you should already know**</td></tr>
<tr><td>

○ the names and properties of polygons
○ how to tessellate 2-D shapes
○ how to make 3-D models

</td><td>

○ How to reflect, rotate and translate shapes
○ How to draw and measure angles
○ How to calculate the angles on a straight line, in a triangle and around a point
○ How to draw nets for 3-D shapes

</td></tr>
</table>

Polygons

A **polygon** is any 2-D shape that has straight sides.

The names of the most common polygons are given in the table below.

Number of sides	Name of polygon
3	Triangle
4	Quadrilateral
5	Pentagon
6	Hexagon
7	Heptagon
8	Octagon
9	Nonagon
10	Decagon

A **convex polygon** has all its diagonals inside the polygon.

A **concave polygon** has at least one diagonal outside the polygon.

Example 18.1 ▷

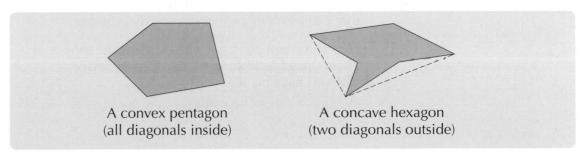

A convex pentagon
(all diagonals inside)

A concave hexagon
(two diagonals outside)

A **regular polygon** has all its sides equal and all its interior angles are equal.

Example 18.2 ▷ A regular octagon has eight lines of symmetry and rotational symmetry of order 8.

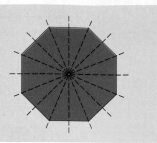

1 Which shapes below are polygons? If they are, write down their names.

a 　　b 　　c 　　d　　e

2 Which shapes below are regular polygons?

a 　　b 　　c 　　d　　e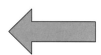

3 State whether each of the shapes below is a convex polygon or a concave polygon.

a 　　b 　　c 　　d 　　e

4 Draw, if possible, a pentagon which has

    a no reflex angles　　　　**b** one reflex angle
    c two reflex angles　　　　**d** three reflex angles

5 Draw hexagons which have exactly

    a no lines of symmetry　　**b** one line of symmetry
    c two lines of symmetry　　**d** three lines of symmetry

6 **a** Write down the names of all the different shapes that can be made by overlapping two squares.

      For example: a pentagon can be made, as shown. Draw diagrams to show all the different shapes that you have made.

    b What shapes can be made by overlapping three squares?

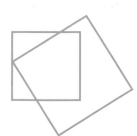

1 Construct a regular hexagon in this way.

a Draw a circle of radius 5 cm.

b With your compasses still set to a radius of 5 cm, go round the circumference of the circle making marks 5 cm apart.

c Join the points where the marks cross the circle using a ruler.

2 A triangle has no diagonals. A quadrilateral has two diagonals.

Investigate the total number of diagonals that can be drawn inside convex polygons.

3 Use ICT to draw regular polygons.

a These instructions describe a square using LOGO:

fd 50 rt 90
fd 50 rt 90
fd 50 rt 90
fd 50 rt 90

b These instructions describe a regular pentagon using LOGO:

repeat 5 [fd 50 rt 72]

Investigate how to draw other regular polygons using LOGO.

Tessellations

A **tessellation** is a pattern made by fitting together the same shapes without leaving any gaps.

When drawing a tessellation, use a square or a triangular grid, as in the examples below.

To show a tessellation, it is usual to draw up to about ten repeating shapes.

Example 18.3

Example 18.4

Example 18.5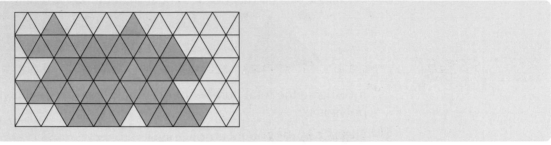

1 Make a tessellation for each of the following shapes. Use a square grid.

a 　　**b** 　　**c** 　　**d**

2 Make a tessellation for each of the following shapes. Use a triangular grid.

a 　　**b** 　　**c** 　　**d**

Extension Work

1 Design a tessellation of your own. Working in pairs or groups, make an attractive poster to show all your different tessellations.

2 Here is a tessellation which uses curves. Can you design a different curved tessellation?

3 Investigate which of the regular polygons will tessellate.

4 Any quadrilateral will tessellate. So, make an irregular quadrilateral tile cut from card. Then use your tile to show how it tessellates.

Constructing 3-D shapes

Construct one or more of the 3-D shapes given in Exercise 18C. For each shape, you start by drawing its net accurately on card.

Make sure that you have the following equipment before you start to draw a net: a sharp pencil, a ruler, a protractor, a pair of scissors and a glue-stick or adhesive tape.

The tabs have been included to make it easier if you decide to glue the edges together. The tabs can be left off if you decide to use adhesive tape.

Before folding a net, score the card using the scissors and a ruler along the fold lines. When constructing a shape, keep one face of the net free of tabs and secure this face last.

Exercise 18C Draw each of the following nets accurately on card. Cut out the net and construct the 3-D shape.

1 **Regular tetrahedron**

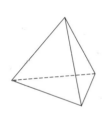
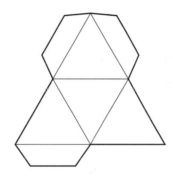

Each equilateral triangle has these measurements:

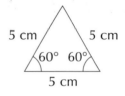

5 cm 5 cm

60° 60°

5 cm

2 **Square-based pyramid**

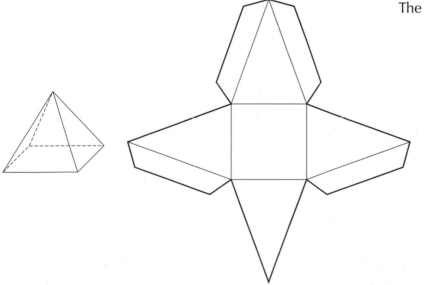

The square has these measurements:

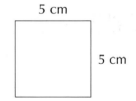

5 cm

5 cm

The isosceles triangle has these measurements:

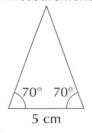

70° 70°

5 cm

3 **Triangular prism**

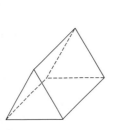

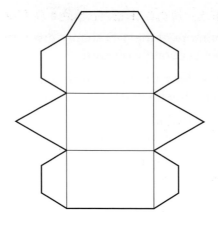

Each rectangle has these measurements:

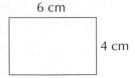

6 cm

4 cm

Each equilateral triangle has these measurements

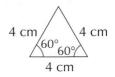

4 cm   4 cm
60° 60°
4 cm

Extension Work

The following nets are for more complex 3-D shapes. Choose suitable measurements and make each shape from card.

1 Octahedron

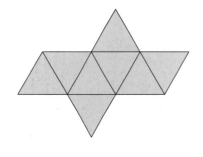

2 Regular hexagonal prism

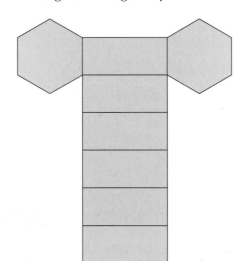

3 Truncated square-based pyramid

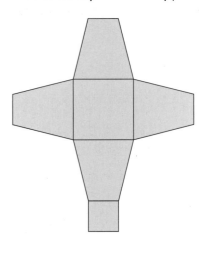

What you need to know for level 4

- The names of and how to draw common 2-D shapes
- How to construct simple 3-D shapes

What you need to know for level 5

- Be able to identify the symmetry of 2-D shapes
- How to use the geometrical properties of 2-D shapes
- How to construct more complex 3-D shapes

LEVEL 4

1 *1993 Paper 2*

Two points are on square dotted paper.

a The points are opposite corners of a square. Draw the square.

b The points are also corners of a bigger square. The corners are both on one side of the bigger square. Draw the bigger square.

LEVEL 5

2 *1993 Paper 1*

Tunde had these six sticks:

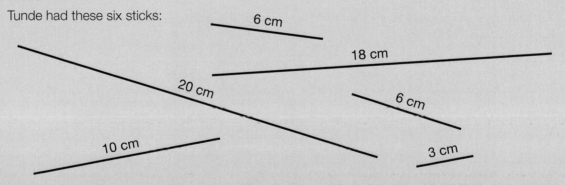

6 cm

18 cm

20 cm

6 cm

10 cm

3 cm

He wanted to make two triangles.

He picked up three sticks. He could not make a triangle with them.

a Which three sticks might Tunde have picked up?

b Why did Tunde's sticks not make a triangle? You can write your answer, or draw a diagram to explain.

Think how you could use all the six sticks to make two triangles.

c Which sticks make the first triangle? Give their lengths.

d Which sticks make the second triangle? Give their lengths.

3 *2000 Paper 1*

The sketch shows the net of a triangular prism.

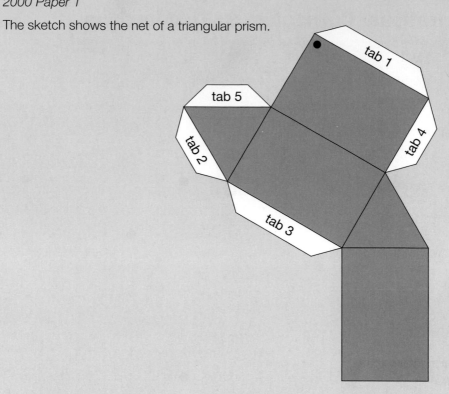

The net is folded up and glued to make the prism.

a   Which edge is tab 1 glued to? On a copy of the diagram, label this edge A.

b   Which edge is tab 2 glued to? Label this edge B.

c   The corner marked ● meets two other corners. Label these two other corners ●.

4   *2001 Paper 1*

The diagram shows a box. Draw the net for the box on a square grid.

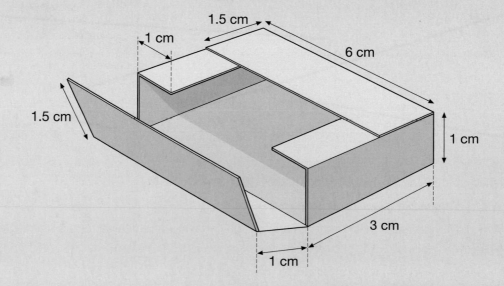